BEYOND CLERICALISM

Scholars Press

Studies in Religious and Theological Scholarship

Christian Identity and Theological Education   Joseph C. Hough, Jr./
John B. Cobb, Jr.

Vision and Discernment: Charles M. Wood
An Orientation in Theological Study

The Arts in Theological Education: Wilson Yates
New Possibilities for Integration

Beyond Clericalism: Joseph C. Hough, Jr./
The Congregation as a Focus for Theological   Barbara G. Wheeler
Education

BEYOND CLERICALISM
The Congregation as a Focus for Theological Education

Edited by
Joseph C. Hough, Jr.
Barbara G. Wheeler

Scholars Press
Atlanta, Georgia

BEYOND CLERICALISM

Edited by
Joseph C. Hough, Jr.
Barbara G. Wheeler

© 1988
Scholars Press

Library of Congress Cataloging in Publication Data

Hough, Joseph C.
    Beyond Clericalism.

    (Scholars Press studies in religious and theological
scholarship)
    Bibliography: p.
    1. Theology--Study and teaching. 2. Parishes.
I. Wheeler, Barbara G. II. Title. III. Series.
BV4022.H59   1988   207'.11   88-24018
ISBN 1-55540-235-6
ISBN 1-55540-236-4 (pbk.)

Printed in the United States of America
on acid-free paper

IN MEMORY OF JAMES F. HOPEWELL

CONTENTS

FOREWORD

Joseph C. Hough and Barbara G. Wheeler

The essays in this volume are, in great measure, a response to the work of the late James Hopewell, who was an energetic and creative participant in the national conversation about theological education. In the late 1970s, Hopewell made a proposal for theological education that represented a rather sharp alternative to current models. In 1983 he circulated the draft of an essay, "A Congregational Paradigm for Theological Education," whose final form appears as the first essay in this book. In it, Hopewell questioned the persistent emphasis on the development of the individual clergyperson as the object of theological education. He noted the shortcomings of the "clerical paradigm" (whose dominance in theological education Edward Farley pointed out and criticized).[1] Hopewell called for a new departure in theological studies, one that would result in "a fundamentally revised curriculum, different both in form and focus, that shifts theological education from a clerical to a congregational paradigm." In this new program the object of theological education would no longer be the formation of the individual minister. Rather, it would be the development of the life and faith of the congregation. The current focus on the formation of the ministerial professional, according to Hopewell, transcends doctrinal and denominational boundaries, and the clerical paradigm has been the basis of virtually all models for theological education, both those in place in actual institutions and those proposed as possibilities for reform. Thus, even the most persistent and imaginative proposals for reform have been, in Hopewell's view, essentially conventional, because they have not questioned the underlying curricular purpose to "form" the individual's character and to teach those skills needed by professional ministers. This means that, in the past, reform had more to do with the changing sociocultural context of ministry than with radical questioning of the individualistic clerical model.

In place of a focus on training persons to provide more effective leadership for established institutions, Hopewell proposed that congregations and ministerial students together attempt to make theologically explicit the life of actual congregations and to empower them to enact their lives in

---

[1] Edward Farley, *Theologia: The Fragmentation and Unity of Theological Education* (Philadelphia: Fortress Press, 1983).

keeping with those theological commitments that undergird the rich symbolic rehearsals of the faith that bind them together and maintain fellowship with other Christian congregations now and in the past. Hopewell's proposal was a formal one. It provided a challenge for rethinking the foundations of theological education, but it left unanswered many questions about both basic concepts and the pedagogical methods appropriate to such a congregational paradigm. Shortly before his death, Hopewell began to organize a project that would address some of those questions.

Hopewell and a small group of fellow theological educators who agreed to act as organizers (including Don Browning, John Cobb, Joseph Hough, David Kelsey and Barbara Wheeler) invited four institutions (the Candler School of Theology, the School of Theology at Claremont, the Yale Divinity School, and Union Theological Seminary in New York) to designate faculty teams that would meet with one another to discuss the effects of making the congregation the central focus of theological education. A series of papers was commissioned for the first gathering of these faculty teams. Some of these papers and several others offered at the second gathering of the faculty groups form the present volume.

The writers, most of them theological educators from the so-called classical fields, were asked to explore the topic from the standpoint of their own disciplines. This direction to look at one's own discipline, the organizers reasoned, might act as a brake on the almost automatic tendency to assign anything to do with ministry to the practical or ministry field, a common move that often reduces discussions of theological study and curriculum to a contention between "theory" and "practice." Thus, Brooks Holifield, for instance, was asked what an intensified focus on the congregation might mean for his teaching of church history in a ministry curriculum. Jane Douglass, Stanley Hauerwas, Beverly Harrison, Don Browning, and others were asked to do the same, substituting their own discipline or field as their point of reference.

The writers were not required to respond directly to Hopewell's proposal that the congregation be viewed as providing a structural paradigm for the curriculum and that the welfare of congregations (rather than individual students) be considered the chief aim of the theological curriculum. Rather, they were urged to write about whatever results they thought could be achieved and would be desirable—or conversely, about any dangers the shift would entail. The papers collected here explore four possible relationships between theological education and the congregation, the two that Hopewell proposed (the congregation serving as a paradigm for and the chief beneficiary of theological education) and two others: Congregations might be viewed as partners of seminaries in the educational process; and they might be treated as a focus for theological studies, as objects and subjects of theological investigations.

It is worth noting that none of the authors chose to write about enhanc-

ing the congregation's most common role in contemporary theological curricula, that of the context or setting for some portion of the student's educational
experience. Two different forms of this idea of the ministry setting as a
context for learning can be found in the various field-based programs offered
in North American seminaries. Many institutions view the congregational
context as a testing ground. Students are cognitively prepared and, in some
traditions, spiritually formed in the crucible of the seminary and then go into
the congregation to learn how to apply theory and to test and develop
personal capacities required in ministry. This conception of the learning
context as a field for the application of theory has recently drawn much
criticism for what have been called its "technical" and "rationalist" assumptions.[2] The critics argue that professional practice usually demands more
than the straightforward application of theory to problems and that in order
to respond adequately to the problems, practitioners must be able to develop
theory, or to search out and synthesize theory developed by others, and to
apply whatever theory has been identified as relevant to a profession's
assigned problems. Practitioners must, in other words, be researchers of a
kind, making observations in action settings and, from them, forming generalizations that structure and explain those observations. Such criticisms have
affected theological education and have led a number of theological educators
to think differently about congregations (and other ministry settings) as
learning contexts, viewing them instead as sources of data for professional
learning as well as, or even more than, testing grounds for theory learned
elsewhere. Neither conception of context, however, seemed to our authors
the most likely or promising path of future development. Unanimously they
chose to describe relationships between the congregation and theological
education that are not currently enacted in schools' actual programs.

I

The papers in the first section of this book take up Hopewell's radical
challenge, that the congregation be conceived as a *paradigm* for theological
education, that is, as a sort of template that could serve to organize the array
of course offerings into a more coherent form. As noted earlier, Edward
Farley contended that theological education is fragmented because it is now
organized according to two patterns, both unsatisfactory. Its fourfold field
structure is, according to Farley, the outworking of a now-discredited pre-
Enlightenment understanding of the church. Within one of the four fields,
the "practical" one, another pattern holds sway: a catalog of clergy functions
that, following Schleiermacher, Farley named the clerical paradigm.[3] Farley

[2] Donald Schön, *The Reflective Practitioner: How Professionals Think in Action* (New York:
Basic Books, 1983).
[3] Farley, *Theologia*, 87.

also suggested, and Hopewell concurred, that living ecclesial reality should provide the fundamental pattern for theological education: Theological education should, in its structure and criteria for what is included and left out, reflect the reality and situation of the church it serves. Hopewell maintained that the congregation—not uniquely, perhaps, but still comprehensively— exemplifies that reality and situation. He thus presented a model of the congregation that he thought could also work as a curriculum pattern.

In the first of his two papers, David Kelsey deals with preliminary matters that must be settled before Hopewell's proposal can be evaluated. For instance, Kelsey questions key terms in the proposal itself. What kind of congregation did Hopewell have in mind? Or, given the diverse forms of church organization, is the focus on *the* congregation a problem? Is it too limited a basis for organizing theological education?

Kelsey suggests that the focus on the congregation could provide a way of avoiding both theological and social-scientific reductionism in the study of the church. Worshiping communities are places where the universal call of God is experienced by a gathered people. The signs and symbols at the center of the congregation's life are reminders that the existence of the church is a gift of God. At the same time, a specific congregation is a reminder of the concreteness of that gift. Therefore, the congregation as the context of thinking about the church provides an incarnational understanding of the church, a perspective necessary for any adequate theological view. The congregation thus helps avoid both ideational and empirical distortions in the discussion of ecclesiology. That in itself, says Kelsey, is sufficient reason to consider making the congregation a focus for theological education.

Kelsey is aware, however, of some troublesome conceptual problems attending the Hopewell proposal and others like it. One of these is the ambiguity of the concept of congregation. A second problem arises out of the first. As soon as one begins to specify what "the congregation" is, one can easily fall into the trap of defining one type of congregation as normative but failing to consider how diverse communities may be. This, in turn, can lead to an ideological distortion of theological education if the congregation is taken as its focus. Finally, a focus on the congregation may not take account of the "ecumenical and catholic character of the church." Kelsey then tries to clarify the conception of the congregation that he believes might avoid some of these problems and thus lead to a definition of the congregation that might make it suitable as a focus for theological education.

John Cobb and Letty Russell are not persuaded by Kelsey's attempt at clarification. From different perspectives, both suggest a "mission paradigm" for theological education and argue that it would have far fewer problems than would the Hopewell proposal, Kelsey's clarification notwithstanding.

Cobb is concerned, as was Hopewell, about the "clericalization" of theological education and the problems it creates for the church, but he believes that a focus on the congregation would only exacerbate the church's tendency to turn inward and to ignore its world mission. This tendency and the accompanying penchant for seeing the congregation's health in terms of institutional maintenance and expansion have become so dominant in our sociohistorical context that we have forgotten that congregations exist to respond to God's call to serve the world. In recent years, theological education has been so profoundly influenced by this inward turning that the ideal of the professional ministry has been distorted. The minister is increasingly seen as one who serves the narrow managerial interests of particular congregations and, to a lesser extent, of wider church organizations.

In this context, Cobb argues, it is almost inevitable that a focus on the congregation would strengthen the hold of the clerical paradigm on theological education. It would, in fact, hinder the needed reform of the idea of the ministerial professional. On the other hand, a focus on mission in and for the world in the seminaries' curricula could help to recast the understanding of professional ministry, by removing many of the distortions of institutionally based clericalism, and it could also help overcome the fragmentation of the theological curriculum.

Letty Russell calls for much the same emphasis to reduce the dominance of clericalism and to resolve the problem of exclusivism in the concept of ministry. She is convinced that the Hopewell proposal or one like it would only increase both these problems, and she contends that it should be rejected on these grounds alone. In addition, she is convinced that there is little chance that any of the so-called academic disciplines outside pastoral theology or practical theology would greatly modify their research or pedagogy to accommodate a congregational focus. Because representatives of these academic disciplines are dominant in theological schools everywhere, Russell thinks that the congregational proposal is politically naive and doomed from the start.

In his second essay, "A Theological Curriculum About and Against the Church," David Kelsey tests the paradigmatic proposal by outlining a curriculum that has the congregation in view. Rather than presenting a model of the congregation, as Hopewell did, to which the curriculum might then be fitted, Kelsey recommends that the curriculum be organized under the headings of two questions about local believing communities. What is the descriptive and normative identity of these communities? And how can this identity be maintained and reformed? The aim of a curriculum constructed in accordance with these questions would "capacitate persons to be learned pastors" but would do it not by focusing on the person of the pastor or the professional minister but by studying "the communal identity of particular Christian churches." It is important to note that Kelsey includes both clergy and laity in his conception of the "learned pastor." Any person who becomes learned about the common life and identity of particular communities may serve as a learned pastor to those communities. Kelsey then sketches the way in which particular courses would be organized to address these questions, noting also how certain kinds of learning would be prominent in the curriculum and how traditional disciplinary courses could be adjusted to the new configuration. In other words, Kelsey provides an outline of a curriculum that accords the congregation paradigmatic significance.

II

In the first section of her paper, Marjorie Suchocki also addresses basic questions. Her focus is not the structure of the curriculum or the theme of individualism, but what she perceives is a theological and a sociological distortion of the image of the congregation in theological education. From a feminist perspective, Suchocki states that the theological problem lies in ecclesiological dualisms that "exalt the ideal church and denigrate the actual church, much like the ideological dualism between Mary and ordinary women." For example, Suchocki sees "the Bride of Christ" image for the church as contributing to both the problem of women in the church and the seminary-church dualism. The implication, she suggests, is that the Godhead relates to the human church as a husband does to his wife. This sexist imagery shapes hierarchical assumptions in relationships between the clergy and laity and between the seminary and church, creating dualistic structures of domination at every point. In this way, the church bears all of the symbolically negative feminine stereotypes in regard to the seminary.

If there is to be a creative relationship between the seminary and the church that it exists to serve, these distortions must be resolved. Suchocki recommends the image of "family friendship" as a model for theological education. By family friendship she means relationships between parents and adult children, a "rich combination of mutuality, friendship and partnership" in which both are parties to the conversation about faith, life, and ministry. An analogue to such family conversations must be created between congregations and theological schools. Family conversation should not remove all distinctions. Both the church and the seminary have distinct roles, but neither is the "object" for the other. Rather, they act together to enrich the ministerial education process.

Thus Suchocki lays the groundwork for her proposal: that the clergy and laity in congregations be *partners* in the educational process alongside theological faculty. The congregation is to become, in other words, a cooperating agent in curriculum and teaching.

Most seminaries have some relationships with congregations that take the form of partnerships. The most common partnership arrangement makes the pastor or other professional leader of a congregation the supervisor of the student assigned to work in that setting. In some field education and internship programs, the supervisory responsibility is extended to a congregational committee that also includes laypersons. Such committees are required in most Doctor of Ministry programs. At the most ambitious end of the part-

nership scale is a type of program in which local leaders are regularly asked
to help provide not only supervision of personal and professional growth but
also formal instruction. In recent decades a number of experimental programs incorporated such intense partnerships (INTERMET was perhaps the
most comprehensive example), but few have survived.

Nor have more modest forms of partnership fared well. Some studies
show that hostility often develops between the supervisory congregational
committees and the seminaries with which they work and that frequently
such committees function poorly.[4] Even the best established form of partnership, the clergy's supervision of seminary students, invites negative criticisms. In many programs, the training of supervisors is haphazard at best,
and their influence is usually quite weak. Thus, even though at least nominal
partnership arrangements are common in theological schools, Suchocki's call
for mutually respectful, productive family alliances between congregations
and theological schools is a proposal for change possibly as radical as the
revisions of basic curricular structures advocated by Kelsey and Hopewell.

III

Closely linked to Hopewell's proposal that the congregation be considered as a curricular paradigm is his suggestion that it might function as the
ultimate *beneficiary* of theological education. This suggestion recognizes that
educational programs are shaped as much by their ultimate purpose as by
their context and by the persons who join in partnerships to conduct them.
To create a curriculum that takes the welfare of local communities of believers
as its goal would thus be a major shift from the curriculum's current orientation to the formation of individual students.

Jane Dempsey Douglass advocates such a conception in the first part of
her paper in a way that makes plain that to do this—to take seriously the
welfare of the congregation—does not mean that seminaries must become
directly involved in educational programs for lay church members. Even if
the congregation's welfare is the final goal, the minister whom the seminary
educates is still a key element in the transaction, and thus the seminary must
continue to pay attention to the formation of that person's competence. But
this formation of the minister can be understood as the middle rather than
the last term in the equation. The final product is the congregation's competence. To take this perspective, Douglass argues, is to ask different ultimate
evaluative questions; not, for instance, whether the curriculum has given its
students a capacity for historical understanding—though the school does
need to know that—but, rather, whether the congregations that seminary

---

[4]See Patricia G. Drake, *A New Look at Lay Training Committees: An Important Role for
Laity in Theological Education* (Washington, D.C.: The Alban Institute, 1979); and Jackson W.,
Carroll and Barbara G. Wheeler, *A Study of Doctor of Ministry Programs* (Hartford, Conn.:
Hartford Seminary, 1986), 107-110.

graduates serve have the historical resources they need—through their minister or by other means—to act faithfully. Obviously, evaluating curricular impact on congregations is difficult, and it can never be conclusive or scientific. But Douglass reports that she has done it: She scrutinizes some of the congregations her students serve and asks whether the congregations themselves are historically equipped for faithful witness and service.

Douglass found that congregations often do not have the historical resources they need. She concludes that the reason for this is that seminaries may not be teaching church history as they must in order to achieve this end. It is not that historical studies are irrelevant but that ministers have not been taught to use the history they have studied. After all, the history of the church, even the history of ideas, is grounded in the churches' concrete life. Any good historical research attends to ideas in context, and those ideas are the products of living congregational realities accompanied by human problems of faith and order. Thus, in principle, the best historical understanding is almost always relevant to contemporary congregational life, and so a revised pedagogy must make this relevance clear. Accordingly, Douglass shows in the second part of her paper how she teaches courses for the congregations' ultimate benefit.

IV

Most of the writers in this volume chose to describe yet another relationship between the congregation and theological education: the possibility that, to a much greater extent than is now the case, the congregation could function as an *object of study*, as a topic that may both be illuminated by the methods of various theological disciplines and also provide useful additions to or slants on the disciplinary subject matter. Taken together, the papers that addressed this challenge—that sketched the consequences of studying the congregation and teaching with reference to it—suggest that the ramifications of doing this would be exceedingly complex and might reach into unexpected areas.

Certainly, the writers do not associate themselves with the conventional wisdom in theological education about where studies of congregations belong in the organization of fields and departments. The general view is that the natural home for congregational studies is in the social sciences: Congregations and other local organizations for ministry are social configurations, and thus one should use sociology to understand their relationships to their environments, organization theory to elucidate how they function as complex systems, psychology to grasp their dynamics, and anthropology and ethnographic research to display them as structures laden with value, symbol, and story. Indeed, this is how congregations are most often studied, but although the social sciences are the research fields in which the study of the congregation has taken root, there are, our writers contend, other promising

arenas. They examine the implications for various fields and often reach the
same conclusion: The scholarship made accessible in seminary courses would
be different—it would have a different shape, emphasis, and perhaps interpretation—if the congregation were accepted as a subject for scholarship,
and, as Douglass suggests, different pedagogies, especially for M. Div.
courses, might emerge in the event of a more central focus on the congregation.

Carl Holladay maintains that modern biblical studies, from the historical-critical movement to the current social-critical and structuralist schools,
have moved closer to the gathered communities that produced the biblical
texts. He begins with a historical overview of research in New Testament
studies and points out that the use of the historical method has been a "drive
for concreteness" that has brought New Testament scholars closer in their
research to actual, local early Christian communities. In other words, the
direction of historical studies of the New Testament may have already paved
the way for a congregational emphasis for scholars in the field. Much the
same could be said about the impact of literary approaches to New Testament
scholarship. Here Holladay notes that the interest in the narrative elements
of New Testament materials may indeed provide a basis for mutually helpful
conversations between New Testament and anthropological scholars about
narrative study in local contemporary congregations. This could help overcome some of the disciplinary isolation of scholars in different fields and
create a richer understanding of the norms and practices of congregational
life. Holladay concludes his review of developments in the discipline by
asserting that a deliberate focus on the congregation might draw together
now disparate methodologies in ways that would make scholarly and pedagogical sense.

Holladay then turns to the impact of a congregational emphasis on the
teaching of the New Testament. He indicates that most recent textbooks for
introductory courses in the New Testament already reflect a shift toward a
congregational focus. Even though advanced exegetical courses present a
different set of problems, Holladay is guardedly optimistic about a possible
congregational focus in those courses too. Though at no point does he deny
the difficulties of relating all New Testament studies to congregational
themes, it is clear that, from his perspective, a congregational emphasis can
be—indeed already has been—accommodated.

Brooks Holifield, writing as an American church historian, finds it odd
that despite the pronounced localism of American religious organizations,
"no one has tried to tell the story of religion in America from a perspective
grounded in the analysis of the congregation." He offers a typology of
American religious congregations that, he believes, cuts across denominational lines. He contends that such a typology, based on an analysis of
congregations, can provide useful insights that supplement more traditional
approaches, altering to some extent both the understanding of the history of

religious institutions in America and the methods of teaching it in theological schools.

Each of Holifield's types—magisterial congregations, sanctuary congregations, and congenial congregations—has a distinct form and function, reflecting doctrinal, social, political, and locational influences. While constructing his typology, Holifield highlights ways in which the understanding of religious movements, theological debates, and sociopolitical changes have influenced congregational life and self-understanding. Such an approach, Holifield states, should not replace the current attempt to teach history in ways that increase the students' self-understanding. It would, however, be an important addition to the history curriculum, one that could give ministers and congregations the conceptual tools for understanding both the historical antecedents of their own congregational forms and the doctrinal assumptions in the missional and liturgical practices they take for granted.

Holifield's approach, then, is demonstrative. He offers an example of the kind of research that might be encouraged by an intensified focus on the congregation as an object of study. He then assesses the benefits of such a move to historical studies, in particular, and to ministerial studies, in general. He is cautiously hopeful about the outcome, provided it does not undermine some key values in the curriculum as it stands.

Can disciplines other than the historical ones also accommodate a new emphasis on the congregation as the object of theological studies? The essays by Don Browning, Stanley Hauerwas, and Beverly Harrison discuss issues in pastoral care and Christian ethics. Both Browning and Hauerwas base their reflections on their participation in and observation of specific congregations. While giving an account of their experiences, they also describe the implications of a congregational focus in theological studies for the disciplines they represent. Harrison, too, draws on her experience in various congregations, particularly as she explores specific pedagogical methods.

In preparing his paper, Don Browning and his students studied how care is actually given and received in local churches. Browning was particularly interested in the forms of care provided by persons and groups other then the professional clergy. Using a method similar to Geertz's "thick description," Browning discovered that pastoral care is often provided mainly by lay members of the congregation to one another and that they find this mutual care to be more meaningful than that provided by the clergy. The members of the church did appreciate the clergy's attention, but they considered such care most effective during major crises or transitions. Browning also discovered that the care that lay members give to one another is not haphazard but is organized in an elaborate network. He thus concludes from his research that a congregational focus could help correct the individualism and psychologism of contemporary pastoral care.

Perhaps Browning's most interesting discovery was that the mode and interpretation of caring seem to be shaped by the social and geographical location of the congregation. Thus, Browning's urban activist church understood both its activism and the discussion and mutual support regarding those activities to be part of its total mutual caring ministry and, by extension, of its ministry to the world around the congregation. In contrast, care was seen quite differently by urban ethnic and suburban congregations. Browning shows how the contextual variables he identifies operate at different levels of reflection, yielding a theology of caring that emerges from the congregation's experiences.

The study on which his paper is based leads Browning to conclude that shifting the focus of theological studies to the congregation would make a difference in methods of research and in the teaching of pastoral care. It would emphasize the importance of "thick description" and, much more than do contemporary approaches, the importance of liturgical ministry as caring ministry. Further, it would stress the importance of context in determining the diverse understandings and forms of pastoral care required in different congregations. In other words, congregational analysis could, in many ways, become more central to research and the teaching of pastoral care in theological schools. Browning's evaluation of such a shift is, therefore, close to Holifield's: The move would enrich research and teaching, but it should not replace more established points of focus and modes of procedure.

Stanley Hauerwas's essay is a reflective theological interpretation of some of his experiences as a participating member of a congregation in South Bend, Indiana. Hauerwas's perspective on the teaching of Christian ethics is already compatible with a congregational approach. For him, the most important assumption for any Christian ethic is that its subject matter is primarily derived from and directed to the faith and life of the church.

Sensitive to critics who accuse him of a misplaced theological idealization of the church, Hauerwas believes that the teaching of Christian ethics must be directed not to deducing moral norms from an ideal vision of the church but to reflecting on the moral significance and the subsequent articulation of moral commitments exposed in the actual decisions of real congregations. That, in Hauerwas's opinion, is the agenda for Christian ethics. The teaching of ethics should be focused on the congregation itself, not simply because it is the church, but also because the minister as a Christian ethicist must be able to discern and explain the theological-moral significance of all of its practice and the connection of that practice to the practice of other congregations, past and present. "The task of Christian ethics is . . . to help the churches tell and share their stories truthfully." For Hauerwas, then, the shift to a congregational focus for theological studies is both possible and necessary for the integrity of the discipline.

Beverly Harrison addresses a different set of issues. She shows how a deeper and more correct understanding of class issues and their ethical implications can emerge from the study of middle class congregations, which she views as disempowered in important but unrecognized ways. Initially,

Harrison asks whether Christian ethics, as she conceives it, is even a discipline. From her vantage point, it is a mosaic of perspectives that must be applied to the normative questions faced by Christians in our current sociohistorical situation. Harrison first analyzes domination as a Christian woman, from a standpoint she shares with liberation theologians. She therefore readily identifies with liberation theology in its approach to "theological-moral" judgments. All such judgments are simultaneously "a normative evaluation of theological–moral social relations." Thus, theological investigations and ethical perspectives always contain at least implicit judgments about social domination, and the normative force of those judgments is not above criticism. What distinguishes Harrison's and others' liberation approaches is their insistence that such criticism is based on the social relations implied by or resulting from such theological and moral formulations. Thus, new theological insight is most likely to emerge from a sociocritical analysis of Christian practice.

One can readily see that like Hauerwas—but for different reasons—Harrison considers the proposed shift toward the congregation as essential to the research and teaching most appropriate to Christian ethics. All Christian ethical reflection should be reciprocal, that is, it is to be "tested and transformed in dialectical relation to the ongoing praxis and faith claims of other believers." Assuming that Christian ethics is interested in human fulfillment, its focus will first be the "unmasking" of all barriers to self-fulfillment, including both exploitation and subjugation. It will then offer suggestions for "resisting" these barriers, a resistance grounded in the resources of the theological-ethical tradition of the Christian community and social theory. These contradictions and the proposals of resistance must be unmasked in the congregations; otherwise the emerging theological-ethical judgments will have no authenticity.

What would a focus on the congregation mean for Christian ethics? For Harrison, it would provide institutional support for the proper function of research and teaching in the discipline. Unless one is able to understand living practice, analyze it, and criticize it from normative perspectives, one cannot do research in Christian ethics, as Harrison defines it. What is true for the researcher is also true for the teacher and the student. To practice Christian ethics requires attention to concrete Christian practice. And because the primary locus of Christian practice is the congregation, a congregational focus is necessary for research, teaching, and learning in a theological school.

V

The essays in this volume are part of a growing body of literature emerging from renewed conversations about theological education in North

America. These conversations, prompted initially by the contributions of Edward Farley, have expanded into the most extensive discussion of the nature and purpose of theological education in recent decades. Farley's book, *Theologia*, became the focus of regional forums of theological faculty and administrators in 1984. Following those discussions, the Association of Theological Schools began a program to extend the breadth and depth of theological reflection on the nature of theological education. That program of Basic Issues Research has involved hundreds of faculty and administrators in research, seminars, and publications. In addition, grants are being made available to promote critical intrainstitutional discussions of patterns of theological education and possibilities for reform.

The interest with which this program has been received, together with the volume of literature produced by the research and discussion during the last decade, indicate a developing consensus among theological faculties and church leadership that theological education must change.[5] Whether this means that theological schools will move toward a paradigmatic reform, as Hopewell suggested, remains to be seen. As Letty Russell points out, neither Hopewell's paradigm nor any other new pattern can be implemented unless historians, biblical scholars, and theologians become convinced that the new model will be related creatively to their disciplinary interests. In fact, all of the disciplines have some vested interests in maintaining the individualistic model of theological education. Discrete disciplines can offer the "theory" necessary to undergird the "practice" of ministry, so that one can simultaneously do well in one's disciplinary research and in teaching, simply by sharing that research as information to influence the formation of future professionals. In this arrangement, there does not need to be tension between one's discipline and the demands of the church for training. The work of the discipline in the university is identified with the function of the discipline in the professional school to provide a "theory" for the profession.

As long as the curriculum's disciplinary organization remains as it is, complaints about the irrelevance of academic theory will continue to encourage a focus on practical skills. This in turn will reinforce the captivity of the minister to the modern professional model, with its focus on managing and counseling at the expense of genuine theological reflection.[6] There is thus a convergence of interest between those who are academic professionals and those who advocate a more "professionalized" clergy in accordance with prevailing cultural norms of professionalism. What all this means, in our view, is that in both the theological school and the church, the current organization of theological studies into a loose confederation of discrete disciplines that focuses on informing the individual student constitutes the

---

[5] Professor Clark Gilpin has complied a selected bibliography of articles and books produced between 1983 and 1987 on basic issues in theological education. The bibliography is available from the Association of Theological Schools.

most critical political fact of life to be faced by those interested in fundamental paradigmatic reform.

It is not surprising, then, that most of the essays in this volume reflect ambivalence with respect to the Hopewell proposal. On the one hand, all of them consider ways in which an increased focus on the congregation is both warranted and, from their disciplinary perspectives, desirable.

David Kelsey and Marjorie Suchocki give whole-hearted assent to Hopewell's proposal. They offer constructive, theologically grounded proposals for total curricular reform, concrete examples of what a "paradigm shift" might look like. Hauerwas and Harrison, though they do not take up the question of governing paradigm, also welcome a shift—in this case, in the focus of studies. Indeed, both believe it necessary to ensure the integrity of their discipline. One could surmise, therefore, that if the whole curriculum moved in the same direction, Hauerwas and Harrison would welcome the support of other disciplines. Browning, Holifield, Douglass, and Holladay all can see ways in which more emphasis on the congregation as the object of theological study could enrich the research and teaching in their disciplines, but they are not enthusiastic about a profound or total shift of attention toward the congregation. That would endanger certain values not present in the curriculum that they wish to preserve. Holifield and Browning explicitly reject a total paradigm shift, but they each demonstrate by example the possibilities for enrichment in teaching and research that they envision when greater attention is given to the congregation as both the object of study and the context of teaching. Only Cobb and Russell reject Hopewell's proposal outright. Neither rejects the idea of a paradigm shift as such. Rather, they argue for a unifying focus for theological education other than the congregation, because they believe that the congregational paradigm has dangers and flaws and is not radical enough.

In summary, the authors in this volume differ about how the congregational proposal should be construed and with what intensity it should be embraced. Nonetheless, the variety and creativity of their analyses and proposals prompt us to suggest that a focus on the congregation that builds in several of the forms of relationship they suggest—partner, beneficiary, and focus of study—is indispensable to making more coherent connections than have been made in the past between theological studies and the practice of ministry. Especially important, we think, is the *study* of congregation for various disciplinary perspectives. Unless students have some historical sense of the relation of the local church communities of the past to broad historical developments; unless they are equipped with a vivid ecclesiological understanding of the local community of believers; unless they grasp the forms ethical issues take for committed communities as well as for individuals; and unless they have some sense of scripture as a testimony of the community's encounter with God, it is unlikely that they will comprehend the full meaning and mandate of Christian leadership in a local congregation. If we persist in representing the tradition as the creation of only high councils and individual geniuses, we cannot be surprised that students have so much trouble linking that tradition to the perplexities of the actual, living, local Christian communities they go out to serve.

Most teachers in theological schools have already incorporated into their teaching some attention to congregations and congregational life. The challenge is to devise strategies for teaching that highlight the moments of learning in which connections are most readily drawn between the tradition and the daily struggles of Christians who gather for worship and service and who maintain and reform those traditions. Students must be prepared to understand the forms in which the living tradition is transmitted in congregational life so that they can lead the churches in appraising the adequacy of their actual witness to the tradition and can create new appropriations of the tradition in their changing contexts.

If there is a need for a congregational focus in teaching, obviously there is also here a challenge for the theological faculties' research agendas. Ideally, good teaching and research should enrich each other. This is one theme persistently emphasized by the writers in this volume. If teaching is to improve the preparation for ministry, the neglect of congregational issues and materials by most of the disciplines in theological studies must be corrected. And as at least three of the essayists in this volume have indicated, this would also lend new excitement to research.

It is, we conclude, probably premature to expect that the conversation about reform in theological education will yield grand answers or a single solution to the problem of coherence and theological integrity. But sometimes incremental changes are tiring and unconvincing, and that is the time for new visions and paradigms to inspire fresh probing and reflection about our common task. This is what Hopewell envisioned, and the essays in this volume indicate that the time is right for just this sort of challenge.

PART ONE
A Congregational Paradigm for Theological Education

A CONGREGATIONAL PARADIGM FOR
THEOLOGICAL EDUCATION

James F. Hopewell

Ian Barbour defined a paradigm as the "tradition transmitted through historical exemplars" that shapes the work of a community of inquiry by providing for it constitutive norms, methodological and metaphysical assumptions, and key concepts.[1] I suggest that the paradigm that now governs the activity of seminaries offering a Master of Divinity program centers on the students' cognitive and characterological development. In this paper I propose that, because of the problems that the current model creates for understanding both theology and ministry, seminaries shift to a paradigm that focus on the local church's cognitive and characterological development.

Edward Farley's term *clerical paradigm* aptly summarizes the premise of today's curriculum,[2] but his characterization[3] of the present mode of that paradigm as functionalist catches only part of the pervasive manner by which it influences the programs of many seminaries. Today schools rely on both functionalist and developmentalist suppositions inherent in the clerical paradigm. The clerical exemplar who motivates and justifies the M.Div. program is not only a professional, functioning by means of technical accomplishment, but also a pilgrim developing toward a ministry never fully to be mastered.

When the study of theology became primarily the academic analysis of the knowledge of God rather than the direct sapiential apprehension of God, Farley argued, the study required a rationale to identify its subject matter and to legitimate its university status. Theology had to prove its function. Its premise was presented by Friedrich Schleiermacher in what Farley termed the clerical paradigm: Theology is necessary for the education of a learned clergy. It is the efficient contribution that the study of scripture, theology, history, and practical theology makes to the ministry of the clergy, and thereby to society at large, that justifies the enterprise of theological education. Although the curriculum has changed since Schleiermacher's justification of its purpose, the old paradigm still holds. Today its functional focus on

---

[1] Ian G. Barbour, *Myths, Models, and Paradigms: A Comparative Study of Science and Religion* (New York: Harper & Row, 1984), 8-11, 102-112.

[2] Edward Farley, *Theologia: The Fragmentation and Unity of Theological Education* (Philadelphia: Fortress Press, 1983), 80-149.

[3] Farley, *Theologia*, 115.

the clergy's "discrete, public tasks"[4]—preaching, counseling, education, social action, and the like—continues to orient the loose assortment of disciplines that now constitute the study of theology.

But the paradigm reflects more than the competencies of ministry. It has also portrayed, at least during this century, the suspicions about competence raised in developmental perspectives on ministry. Images of the minister as a wounded healer or community symbol, expressing the condition of ministry more than its accomplishment, act to modify the curriculum's identification with ministerial professionalism. Concern for religious nurture and the clinical movement express the paradigm's partial grounding in developmentalist images.

The clerical paradigm that justifies the current seminary program projects a student who is to serve both functional and developmental ends, a person who measures up to church comprehensions of ministry (tested by tools like Readiness for Ministry and ordination examinations) but who is also self-aware and self-possessed (processive qualities probed in such structures as clinical supervision and seminary advisory relationships). Thus when curricula are revised, courses proposed, or ordinands counseled about their programs, it is usually the blended intention of student competence and maturation that figures the argument. A mixed image of professional service to the church and of personal growth characterizes seminary catalogs, teaching strategies, and graduation addresses.

As Farley pointed out, the clerical paradigm creates a number of undesirable consequences. I shall describe two and show how both functional and developmental aspects of the paradigm contribute to each problem.

One result is the dispersion and fragmentation of the theological curriculum into a growing assortment of topics and tactics. A paradigm that warrants courses because of their contribution either to the competence or the maturation of a student is hospitable indeed to such dispersion. New skills felt essential to ministry as well as new forms of learning crowd the curriculum and compromise its coherence. The new approaches do not merely cash out in the better functioning of ministry; they also enrich the development of the student as a human being and are thus authorized as curricular elements along with topics of more patent technical value. Although both developmental and functional contributions may benefit student and church, the novel skills and understandings nevertheless disintegrate the formal unity of a curriculum and undermine its integrity as an educational program distinct in its progression and closure.

Another consequence of the clerical paradigm is its promotion of an individualistic understanding of ministry. Despite occasional discussions in courses about the corporate ministry of the community of faith, a M. Div. program centers on the biography and professional profile of the particular

---

[4] Farley, *Theologia*, 115.

student, who as a single executor internally integrates the topics of the program and later applies them to social contexts like congregations that are, in this view, less active in ministry. The problems of a curriculum built on the individualism of the clerical paradigm again have functional and developmental aspects. Both the competence and the maturity required for ministry are judged to exist more reliably in the single leader. But the reduction of ministry to clerical performance impedes the church's reformation. The functionalist concentration on the pastor's competence avoids more radical questions about the faithfulness and utility of Christian ministry as a whole and makes Christian service a matter of fulfilling norms and practicing techniques already defined and adopted by the church. Even more serious is the consequence of the developmental aspect of the clerical paradigm, which suggests the primacy of a student's personal faith journey and thus obscures the process and quality of the community's own redemptive quest. Hence the clerical paradigm encourages solipsism in its participants, implying that ministry originates within the self and affects the world by means of the individual's own action.

Theological education conducted on the basis of the clerical paradigm persists despite its shortcomings. It is the least expensive and best understood of the educational options, perhaps because it reflects so well the present culture's values. Robert Bellah typified American society's turn away from earlier communal values to the individualistic aims of management and psychotherapy. In his address to the Association of Theological Schools in 1982, he challenged theological education to counter the prevailing functionalist and developmentalist ethos, and he pondered the extent to which churches and seminaries have themselves succumbed to its power:

> We must consider how we can reappropriate under contemporary conditions authentic religious and ethical models of human existence, models that will provide vigorous alternatives to the domination of bureaucratic individualism. Here we will have to survey existing resources as embodied in the actual churches, though we will also have to consider the extent to which the churches themselves are run by managers and have accepted the idea that their primary function is therapy. (We might also consider how much this same pattern is found in the theological schools themselves.)[5]

Compromised by its culture-bound proclivities and crippled by its curricular fragmentation and bias toward the individual, the current pattern of theological education requires major adjustment. I shall sketch one channel for change.

---

[5] Robert N. Bellah, "Discerning Old and New Imperatives in Theological Education," *Theological Education* 19 (Autumn 1982): 18.

The Proposal

I advance the idea of a fundamentally revised curriculum, different in both form and focus, that shifts theological education from a clerical to a congregational paradigm. The program's main object would be the development of the congregation, not of the student.

The proposal is not necessarily a plea for more contextual or field education in the curriculum, or one that advocates a greater proportion of pastoral theology courses. Such measures by themselves cannot change a program's fix on the individual. Even the more ambitious experiments in contextual education seldom analyzed and addressed as their basic responsibility the transformation of the community. Rather, contextual placements have functioned as laboratories in which developing students are supervised.

Nor is the proposal necessarily an argument for a closer institutional alignment between the seminary and the church. The mutually critical relationship between the academy and its ecclesiastical partner is essential to an education that seeks to serve the interest of congregations. If the church and the theological school adopt the same norms and perspectives, each institution will lose its prophetic and constructive power.

Instead, the proposal seeks an accomplishment deeper than a physical or political association. It aims to join seminary and congregation in a quest for the redemptive community. It lays upon each partner the responsibility, now consigned to the church in general, to pursue the means by which a particular group of human beings gathered in the name and power of Christ in fact work together to fulfill the Christian promise. The seminary is not permitted merely to prepare the individual who might later guide the local church in the quest, nor is the local church allowed to assign its own responsibility for the quest to a clergyperson so prepared.

There are no pedagogical models in other professional and technical fields for the education envisioned here. Legal education, if it sought a just community rather than skill in litigation and negotiation, might be an example, as would medical education if its object were a healthy society rather than the healing of certain categories of sickness. More proletarian institutions like commercial and police academies sink even deeper into technical routines that do not explore the point and welfare of the systems they serve. Education in the humanities often has the necessary scope and breadth, but usually it lacks a specific community as the object of its concern for human welfare. At best one can draw only hypothetical examples from other fields of training. Their institutions appear, despite their own reformers, to have been captured as much as theological education has in forms of bureaucratic individualism.

The Object of Theological Education

What if, for example, maritime education took as its object of concern the welfare, orientation, and travel of ships, not merely the training of officers? Although mates and engineers are essential to the purpose, their education would not be focused on getting themselves to port; it would be to get the ship to port.

A congregation is a sort of ship, and its welfare and destination, as far as the congregation controls them, lie in its self-understanding and moral development. Although the same might be said of other agencies of Christianity, the local church is proposed as the object of theological education because it is the nearest at hand to the seminary and the primary community in the careers of theological students. Focusing on the congregation, however, is more than a pedagogical convenience. The local church also exhibits an unusual capacity to reflect the struggle of human society and the theological and ethical issues that emerge in this struggle.

The concentration of a curriculum on congregations might appear to some to be constricting and to avoid issues in Christian social action better expressed in global and class terms. I think the opposite. Issues considered in their generalities tend to remain the nonspecific topic of councils, documents, and conferences. But issues require grounding in particular circumstances. The more I study the congregation and its immediate context, the more clearly I see in it the embodied instance of human participation in power and pluralism, in oppression and absurdity, and in struggles against their bane. To focus on the culture and structure of the local church is to participate locally in a much larger venture into how human societies everywhere labor to communicate and liberate themselves. Focusing on the local church is subversive. This apparent act of self-reference brings to consciousness the symbolic and social processes that underlie both the gathering and the cleavage of all humanity.

Addressing the congregation also evokes a quite different notion of pedagogical effectiveness. When the consuming object of teaching is to develop a student's career, there is need for fast, decisive action: The object then is to impart a quick progression of concepts and behavior patterns before a graduation that comes all too soon. The urgency requires that many issues be only simulated and described, not experienced, which creates special problems of dislocation and irrelevance of education to actual church life. An educational bond between seminary and congregations, however, could be more sustained and symbiotic, less given to artificial rhythms and climaxes in learning. The effect of inquiry and teaching would be more cumulative than summary, more dialectical than programmatic. As in a teaching hospital, students would participate in an ongoing, larger labor for comprehension and praxis. Their own stay, although having a curriculum, would be more tangibly set in activities pursued before and beyond their personal involvement.

Knowing the Vessel

Following the managerial and therapeutic bent of our times, most of those writing about the local church have produced rather superficial works that promote efficient operation or improve interpersonal relations. Such efforts serve a clerical paradigm in which pastors need tools to apply their learning to the practical needs of the congregation. The manner of their application is to perceive, again in keeping with the times, the congregation as a loose congeries of individuals who need professional assistance for technical alignment in church programs or psychic cohesion in church fellowship. The clerical paradigm thus deprecates the congregation and denies the church's social reality as a bodied community that coheres by means of its own "thick" culture. The culture of any congregation, in fact, sustains and digests the ministrations of its clergy.

Theologically trained personnel are essential to the church, but they are to serve Christian groups who are like ships. Congregations are the tubs, trawlers, and love boats of Christianity: highly complex, cybernetically sufficient vessels of crew and apparatus given to data, story, and other symbolic interaction. The relation of education to the ship should not be one in which the school generates theories and graduates who put theories into practice on passive craft. In its sailing, the vessel uses its own intelligence and recalls and plays out its own story. Education is a response to that salty experience.

Fortunately, the local church has now been examined more thoroughly than the books on its management and therapy suggest. In recent years the approaches of cultural anthropology and community sociology have begun to explore the layers of meaning and social process at work in particular congregations. Samuel Heilman's study of a synagogue[6] and Melvin Williams's analysis of a poor black church[7] are examples. Now an increasing number of Ph.D. dissertations are ethnographic studies of congregations.[8] Steven Tipton's examination of the world view and ethos of a charismatic church shows how descriptive ethics can uncover the moral culture of a congregation.[9] Investigations of the social worlds and behavior patterns of church members have been standard fare in sociological journals for two decades.[10]

By giving its attention to the local church's cultural process, the semi-

---

[6] Samuel C. Heilman, *Synagogue Life: A Study of Symbolic Interaction* (Chicago: University of Chicago Press, 1973).

[7] Melvin D. Williams, *Community in a Black Pentecostal Church: An Anthropological Study* (Pittsburgh: University of Pittsburgh Press, 1974).

[8] Nancy T. Ammerman, "The Fundamentalist World View: Ideology and Social Structure in an Independent Fundamental Church" (Ph.D. diss. Yale University, 1983); Michael Ducey, *Sunday Morning: Aspects of Urban Ritual* (New York: Free Press, 1977).

[9] Steven M. Tipton, *Getting Saved from the Sixties: Moral Meaning in Conversion and Cultural Change* (Berkeley and Los Angeles: University of California Press, 1982).

[10] Summaries of sociological analyses of the congregation appear in Jackson W. Carroll, William McKinney, and Wade Clark Roof, "From the Outside In and the Inside Out: A Sociological Approach," in *Building Effective Ministry: Theory and Practice in the Local Church*, ed. Carl S. Dudley (San Francisco: Harper & Row, 1983), 89-111; and Carl S. Dudley and James F. Hopewell, "Understanding and Activating Congregations: A Bibliography," in Dudley, *Building Effective Ministry*, 246-256.

nary concentrates on how the community itself links theory and practice in a complex system of signals. Not only does the congregation act; it also—by means of symbol, story, and technique—examines its behavior. The congregation is not, as curricula built on the clerical paradigm seem to suggest, merely the field on which ministry is played out. By its own "webs of significance" (Geertz), the local church itself gives entity and significance to what it does.

A theological program focused upon the life and development of the congregation could thus discover within its primary subject the phenomena that disclose both the practice and theory of the church. Virtually everything that happens in a congregation is a symbolic interaction. James Gustafson called such a group a "community of language," and for a school to probe that language would help it understand the tissue that holds together humanity's expression and performance.

Theology and Education

Accepting the implications of a congregational paradigm for theological education would launch both seminary and church into a tentative, fragile venture. Both would undergo, and test, the institutional consequences of treating a congregation as a community of faith whose particular life can be made theologically explicit. Instead of considering themselves the ultimate beneficiaries of a remote seminary process, congregations would be encouraged to understand their generative role in theological education. Part of the seminary's responsibility would be to provide reason and means for a church's growing awareness of this role. The present relation between theological education and Christian education would thus require reconstruction in a manner that effectively linked theological inquiry to the maturation of a community. No satisfactory models for that endeavor now exist, and indeed, this paper is more a call for its construction than its blueprint.

Teachers who would like to experiment might try the path incompletely blazed by Ernst Troeltsch. Troeltsch sought to discover the redemptive presence of Christ in the life of specific worshiping communities for whom Christ was the "support, center, and symbol."[11] The essence of Christianity, according to his inquiry, was not to be found in philosophical reflection or in mystical encounter but within the ongoing existence of the cultic community. It was that group, Troeltsch argued, that first authenticated the person of Christ and that has since preserved the centrality of Jesus in its history of worship and self-identification. Troeltsch saw the necessity of discerning the apprehension of God as it occurs in concrete, corporate circumstances.

[11] Ernst Tröltsch, *Die Bedeutung Geschichlichkeit Jesu fur den Glauben* (Tubingen: J.C.B. Mohr-Paul Siebeck, 1911). Translated in Robert Morgan and Michael Pye, *Ernst Troeltsch: Writings on Theology and Religion* (Atlanta: John Knox Press, 1977), 202.

How would the labor of congregations and their partner seminaries, engaged together in a quest for the redemptive life, differ from the present concern for management and therapy? Possibly the major contrasts would appear in the intensity of the struggle to understand the context and identity of the individual congregation, and the contribution of theology to that understanding. The dimensions of social context and corporate identity languish in current conceptions of ministry and its education, and the appropriation of a congregational paradigm would necessitate their recognition.

Instead of dealing primarily with abstractions of "the world," "the church," and "the people," a congregational approach to church *context* would determine how such entities exist in a local church's particular area. Bracketing, as a good ethnographer might, preconceived conclusions about social meaning and process, the theological inquiry would be directed to finding out how church and world are in fact instantiated in a particular place, what forms the historical and ecumenical context of a local church, what makes the church local, and what constitutes its human situation and informs its response as a church. Only by understanding its larger social matrix can a church recognize its own congregating and its consequences. The commitment of a theological faculty to probe a particular congregation's context would reintroduce in a fresh way its best historical and ethical methods.

Discerning the *identity* of the congregation would necessitate a similarly intense inquiry. Examining the life of a specific local church would dispel the notions that scripture and theology are automatically the heritage or story of actual churches. Rather, the matter is more complicated, involving issues of continuity and discontinuity, of culture and Christ, of revelation and history—all the biblical and theological conundrums lurking in microcosmic form in an embodied community that dares to call the body Christ's. For a theological faculty to share responsibility for understanding a congregation's identity would plunge it into the languages of a church's association, there to ponder—by means of its disciplined approaches to scripture and theology— the symbolic interaction by which a community of believers forms its singular sense of who they together are.

The *tasks* of ministry to which management and therapy respond would require further attention, because it is through planned programs and interpersonal processes that perceptions are transmitted and corporate actions occur. A Christian community lives not only in its given context and according to perceptions of its identity but also by its labor to further its purpose. Such corporate labor requires attention to planned activities and the dynamics of development. In a congregational paradigm, however, the functions and therapies of ministry would be regulated by the goals and values discovered in studies of the Christian church's context and identity. Explorations to establish the moral dimensions of practical theology are critical to the alignment of theological education with the life of the local church.

Obviously the future task would involve much of its own definition. Goals, rather than elaborated means, now justify this new paradigm. The goals are a corporate form of learned ministry, an education not once removed from the church's embodiment, a concurrence of church and academy in the struggle for specific redemptive community.

ON THE CHRISTIAN CONGREGATION

David H. Kelsey

To focus theological education on the study of the congregation, as James Hopewell suggested, is an interesting proposal because the congregation, in its concreteness, might provide a way to hold in check both social-scientific reductionism and, equally important, theological reductionism in the study of any topic in theological education. In his essay on the church, *Treasure in Earthen Vessels* (1961), James Gustafson acknowledged that a purely social-scientific account of the church is reductionist and inadequate. Moreover, he pointed out, an account of the church cast solely in theological terms is, in its own way, just as reductionist and inadequate. Furthermore, Gustafson seemed to argue, theological reductionism is inadequate on theological grounds.

A theological description insists that the church is God's gift and not simply a human device. It insists that the church's *raison d'être* is a mission to which God calls it and not simply the pursuit of human interests, that God has promised to be present in the church and through it to the world, without denying that God's grace is also present to others in quite different settings. At the same time, a theological account of the church insists that all this is said of a company of persons that always has a particular geographical, historical, cultural, social, and political location. On theological grounds, this last claim means that an account of the church is inadequate if it is not also receptive to social-scientific accounts. The church may be a place where God is present to human life, but it is a concrete place. A theological description and a scientific description of the church refer to the same concrete reality, not to separate parts of it, and certainly not to two different realities. The church must be described and understood in an "incarnational" way. Such incarnational patterns of thought are characteristic of Christianity. Accordingly, a focus on the congregation as the context in which other topics in theological education (besides "the church") are studied may help check a drift toward theological and social-scientific reductionisms, each of which is inadequate to an incarnational way of thinking. This is a large part of what makes a focus on the study of the congregation an interesting proposal for the possible reform of theological education.

But it is precisely the concreteness of congregations that makes Hopewell's proposal problematical to so many. In this paper, I shall explore the problems that Hopewell's proposal creates and then develop a definition of the congregations that may answer some of the objections. There are at least three ways in which the proposal is troubling. First, the very concreteness of congregations makes the concept of congregation seem indefinite. To what concrete companies of human beings does congregation refer? What counts as a congregation?

One problem is whether the word *congregation* is to be used in a cross-cultural way. In many European and Latin American cultures with established church traditions (whether by law or by social convention) a congregation is identified with a parish. In that case, *parish* designates a geographical area in which every resident is a member of the congregation unless (in some nations) he or she is in some way exempted. A person is considered a member of the congregation simply by living in the parish. In this concept of congregation, a person is considered a member of the company of the parish/congregation even if he or she never entered the local church building between baptism as an infant and last rites at death or ever joined with other members of the parish in church-related activities. Even so, it can be argued that the local parish is important to the lives of such nonparticipant parishioners and so shapes their identities that they are genuinely "members" of the one "body" of the parish/congregation.

By contrast, in North America congregations are composed of persons who openly identify with a particular company of Christians. This is true even of congregations that continue to describe themselves as parishes. In this context, parish may designate a geographical area from which a congregation is entitled to draw its members, but parish no longer designates a territorially defined population assumed to comprise the congregation. In this concept of congregation, a person is considered a member of the body of the congregation only as a result of some deliberate act of self-identification with it.

When we speak of making the study of the congregation a focus of theological education, will congregation refer to both of these kinds of parish? If we decide to use congregation only in the second sense, we shall need to make clear that our proposal is focused on a characteristically North American mode of church and therefore may have a limited application to other cultural settings.

In the North American concept of congregation, the term is customarily used to refer to an organized, residentially based group of Christians, a group that often belongs to one of several national denominations. But congregation is also used to refer to a group of persons who actually congregate on a given occasion for worship. The first meaning of congregation encompasses various activities that endure through time. Its members vary in the time, energy, and resources they spend in the congregation's common life.

The second meaning of congregation lasts only as long as the activity for which it gathered lasts. Such a congregation usually includes members of the former, to whom may be added visitors, some of whom may never again join with the others in any way for any purpose. Between these two kinds of congregations are other kinds of companies of Christians: staff, patients, and friends of patients gathered for worship in a hospital; companies of Christians gathered for brief periods for study, for ecumenical discussion, or for church governance; or groups of Christians gathered because of their commitment to a project, for example, protest and resistance to particular foreign policies. When we speak of making the study of the congregation a focus for theological education, to which congregation are we referring? A congregation is concrete. But unless it is specifically identified, its range of referents is so indefinite that its use is bound to be confusing.

A second concern about making the congregation a focus of theological education is closely related to the first. Let me use the example of a suburban mainline Protestant congregation as a paradigm. Surely it is a signal of ideological bias, if, in the North America context, one identifies a Christian congregation with companies of Christians whose major criterion of self-selection is that they live in the same kinds of neighborhoods. Because neighborhoods tend to be economically and socially homogenous, so their residents tend to be shaped by and to reflect the interests peculiar to their particular economic and social location. And those interests can distort, among other things, the way in which the church's nature and purposes are understood and enacted. Hence the concrete reality of such congregations will be ideologically skewed. In this cultural setting, is it really possible to invoke the congregation as a focus for theological education without also giving pride of place to an ideologically distorted load of meaning one would wish rather to denounce?

The concreteness of congregations causes a third reservation about the proposal to make their study a focus of theological education. An adequate theological description of the church would insist that it is greater than any local congregation. And an adequate scientific description of the church would insist that any local congregation is part of a greater social and cultural context. Accordingly, this third concern is two-sided: Because of the congregation's concrete particularity, a focus on it in theological education may obscure both the ecumenical and the catholic character of the church and the ways in which the congregation is shaped by its social and cultural context.

I shall propose some ways to clarify the concept of congregation in regard to its use in theological education.

The Referents of the Christian Congregation

What counts as a Christian congregation? We might answer: Any group of persons that gathers to worship God in the name of Jesus. The phrase "in the name of Jesus" draws attention to at least three features of groups denoted by the expression "Christian congregation," one descriptive and the other two normative.

Throughout the history of the Christian movement, the worship of God has assumed a distinctive social form, and accordingly, a congregation is a social form distinguished by its social space. Hopewell's definition is helpful: "A congregation is a group that possesses a special name and recognized members who assemble regularly to celebrate a more universally practiced worship but who communicate with each other sufficiently to develop intrinsic patterns of conduct, outlook, and story."[1] That is, a congregation is a group with a communal identity. The distinctiveness of its social space is largely a function of the medium by which its members communicate with one another and the end to which they communicate. The various activities through which this communication takes place (worship, preaching, prayer, counsel, education, self-governance) constitute the group's common life. The medium in which these kinds of communication take place consists largely of biblical images, metaphors, and narratives. And this medium is used in the activities comprising the community's common life to help shape and even transform the personal identities of the group's members in ways that accord with the group's communal identity. This is a shaping of their identities as agents, or embodied centers of power, as much as it is a shaping of them as patients, or centers of consciousness. The characteristic social form of Christian worship, then, has generally consisted of a social space that is moral and even political in character, a space defined and structured by power relationships. But this definition has not always been acknowledged, let alone approved or celebrated. Nonetheless, as Wayne Meeks showed, this was true even of congregations of the earliest urban Christians.[2]

As Hopewell pointed out, such "congregations are only one of several sorts of collectivities by which humans corporately express their religion."[3] It is by no means obvious that the congregation should be the characteristic social form of Christian worship, but the fact that it is, is because Christian worship is done "in the name of Jesus."

For example, worship can be focused by family loyalties, honoring ancestors and negotiating critical transitions in a family's life cycle. Something like this often overlies Christian worship, especially at Easter and Christmas, when unusually large groups gather less to celebrate the church year than to express loyalty to family and reverence for its traditions. But as Hopewell stated, "A congregation differs from a family at prayer. The local

[1] James F. Hopewell, *Congregation: Stories and Structures* (Philadelphia: Fortress Press, 1987), 12-13.

[2] Wayne Meeks, *The First Urban Christians: The Social World of the Apostle Paul* (New Haven, Conn.: Yale University Press, 1983).

[3] Hopewell, *Congregation*, 14.

church bears a distinctive name to indicate . . . that the congregation is not synonymous with a particular bond of flesh."[4]

Another common social form of worship is the collective piety of political units—a town, a nation, an empire. Clearly, from Constantine onward, congregations in Western Christendom have been threatened by assimilation into this different social form. Equally clearly, the fact that the worship of God transpires "in Jesus' name" has kept alive guilt regarding such assimilation and a memory that the congregation's distinctive name means that it is not synonymous with any bond of compatriotism.

Hopewell draws attention to two more forms of religious assembly that are found in Asia and differ from the social form of Christian worship. One is a type of corporate observance that occurs at a shrine or other holy place:

> In these settings a small corps of priests or other functionaries . . . provides ceremonial proficiency and continuity for a larger lay populace whose participation . . . tends to be more . . . occasional and informal. . . . Most worshipers at a shrine on a single day do not communicate sufficiently with each other to develop the unique pattern of conduct, outlook and story that distinguishes the local congregation.

The other type of religious assembly consists of lay followers of a Buddhist monastic order, the *sangha*. They "may gather in groups to perform meritorious rituals of devotion at the monastery, but their participation is individual and limited, unlike the congregation of monks whose corporate life they support."[5] Although both of these forms of religious assembly involve groups of persons, they perform simultaneous individual acts of worship rather than a single act of worship by a group with a strong community identity. Once again, the characteristic social form of Christian worship seems to be worship by a congregation that has a distinctive name and a shared community identity and acts as a whole.

The descriptive fact that the worship of God "in Jesus' name" has brought with it this characteristic social form requires a modification of our answer to the question, What counts as a Christian congregation? Now we may answer: Any group of persons who gathers to worship God in Jesus' name regularly enough for an indefinite period of time to have a common life in which develop intrinsic patterns of conduct, outlook, and story.

In our description of what counts as a Christian congregation, the phrase "in Jesus' name" is normatively as well as descriptively decisive. By explicitly engaging in the communal worship of God in Jesus' name, a group both acquires a distinctive name and identity and adopts a criterion by which to

---

[4] Hopewell, *Congregation*, 13.
[5] Hopewell, *Congregation*, 14.

distinguish Christian from non-Christian gatherings to worship. That a group explicitly worships God in Jesus' name is a necessary condition of its being a Christian congregation.

Even though "in Jesus' name" is a necessary condition of a congregation's "Christianness," it does not necessarily mean that it is a sufficient condition. Whether it is sufficient and, if not, what additional conditions must be met are matters of continuing theological controversy. The practices and attitudes of some Christian congregations toward other self-described Christian congregations at least suggest that the first group of congregations differs from the latter on this question. But what the necessary condition does establish is the circle of groups entitled to engage in the controversy, namely, all of those who explicitly assume the self-identification of "in Jesus' name." It is important to recall that one of the fruits of the ecumenical movement is the growing consensus that there probably should be no more criteria beyond the intent to worship God in Jesus' name.

This necessary condition does not require any particular answer to questions about whether God is truly known and worshiped by groups who do not worship in Jesus' name or whether God is redemptively present to them. A discussion of those questions must draw on other theological convictions beyond the scope of this paper. Our necessary condition does mean, however, that any congregation that does assume this name and identity thereby also affirms that there is a difference between Christian and non-Christian congregations and that this difference matters. It matters because both the character of the group's communal identity and the way it shapes its members' personal identities are at stake.

The normative force of "in Jesus' name" as a necessary criterion of a congregation's Christianness brings with it another modification of our answer to the question, What counts as a Christian congregation? Now, as a third approximation, we may answer: Any group of persons that gathers to worship God regularly enough for an indefinite period of time to have a common life in which develop intrinsic patterns of conduct, outlook, and story and explicitly do so "in Jesus' name" as a deliberate act of self-identification.

The phrase "In Jesus' name" is decisive in a third way. If a group of persons worships God "in the name of Jesus," it not only assumes a particular communal identity, but it also adopts a criterion by which its patterns of conduct, outlook, and story can be assessed. To worship God in Jesus' name is to worship God in ways intended to be faithful to Jesus' However, the group's conduct, outlook, and story may turn out not to be faithful to Jesus' name. Exactly what it means to worship God in patterns of conduct, outlook, and story that are faithful to Jesus' mission and God's mission in Jesus depends on the particular understandings of Jesus and his relation to God, that is, the material content of a Christology.

What is to be noted here is the possibility of simultaneously having a particular identity and being faithless to it. A congregation may be truly "Christian," that is, deliberately assumes the communal identity that goes with worshiping God in Jesus' name, while at the same time be in some ways faithless to Jesus' name. Such a congregation may be "Christian" but "sinful." Whether this is judged to be a real or only a conceptual possibility depends on other theological commitments, principally beliefs regarding the nature of Christian existence. There are several possible views. One is a perfectionist view, according to which any group that fails to be faithful to what is implied in identifying itself by reference to Jesus also fails to count as a Christian congregation. Presumably the group's contrary avowals of its intent to worship God in Jesus' name must be rejected as insincere or self-deluded.

According to a second view, an explicit avowal of intent to worship God in Jesus' name simply constitutes faithfulness, no matter how successfully the intent is carried out in action. Each view is probably an unrealistic extreme, however, as actual theologies of Christian existence, for all their diversity, generally acknowledge some version of a real and not simply a conceptual distinction between having a Christian identity and being faithless to it.

This brings with it a modification of our answer to the question, What counts as a Christian congregation? As a fourth approximation, we may answer, Any group of persons that gathers together to worship God; that explicitly does so "in Jesus' name" as a deliberate act of self-identification; that does so regularly enough for an indefinite period of time to have a common life in which develop intrinsic patterns of conduct, outlook and story; and that holds its common conduct, outlook, and story accountable regarding its faithfulness to Jesus' mission and God's mission in Jesus. This may help define the range of possible referents denoted by the phrase "the Christian congregation" when the study of the congregation is used as the focus for theological education and thus may answer the first concern, the indefiniteness of the phrase.

The Ideological Congregation

The second problem about making the study of the congregation central to theological education is that the residentially based congregations characteristic of North American Christianity are ideologically distorted. Thus if such congregations are made the context in which other theologically important matters are studied, this will skew the entire theological enterprise.

The fact of the congregation's ideological captivity is not in question. Indeed, it is true in at least two senses. In our discussion of the phrase "Christian congregation," we noted that part of the descriptive force of defining Christian congregations as groups gathered in Jesus' name is that they characteristically have a common life marked by intrinsic patterns of conduct, outlook, and story. In every instance, those patterns of conduct, outlook, and story are shaped by the group's host culture and by the group's social, political, and economic location in its host society. This means that every congregation's patterns of conduct, outlook, and story will be ideologically shaped by the interests central to its social location.

It also means that some, but not all, congregations' patterns of conduct, outlook, and story will be ideological in a second, narrower sense. These are congregations whose social location is determined by that population of the host society that benefits materially and in some (but not all) respects psychologically from unjust social, economic, and political structures by which other segments of the population are disempowered and oppressed. These are congregations whose patterns of conduct, outlook, and story are shaped by interests that would be hurt if the society's unjust structures were reformed. However subtly, these interests tend to shape such a congregation's view of its mission in ways that obscure injustice in its host society or subvert efforts to secure justice. The failure to recognize this and to struggle against it is sinful rather than inevitable. Whereas all congregations are in some respect ideologically biased in the first sense of ideological— simply because of a congregation's concrete incarnation in some society and culture—in the second sense of ideological only some congregations may be ideologically distorted.

Does this ideological distortion of congregations disqualify them as the focus of theological education? We can divide the question on the basis of a distinction we noted earlier, that the phrase "in Jesus' name," as used to define Christian congregations, has two kinds of normative force. "In Jesus' name" is a self-definition of a group's identity as a *Christian* congregation, and it names the criterion by which the group's faithfulness to its identity can be assessed. Thus, does the ideological distortion of the congregation disqualify it as a Christian congregation, and does the ideological distortion of the congregation exhibit its faithlessness?

I think we should be cautious about denying the Christianness of any congregation on the grounds of its ideological bondage in either the broad or the narrow sense of ideological. The reason for this is as follows: The Christian congregation is a group that gathers to worship God in the name of Jesus, in ways that are shaped as a response to the biblical stories about Jesus' own mission and God's mission in Jesus. This response has two sides. On the one hand, the response is an adoration of God, central to which are acts of grateful and joyous celebration of the stories of God's mission in Jesus among and on behalf of humankind. On the other hand, the response consists of works of love for one's neighbor. These two responses are different and yet inseparable. The adoration of God and works of love must be shaped by biblical stories concerning Jesus' mission and God's mission in Jesus. Hence, the actions in which the adoration of God and works of love are carried out must include a self-critical assessment of their adequacy as responses to the biblical stories. At the same time, in actual practice, the adoration of God and works of love are also made concretely actual in the languages of speech and significant behavior that are made available by a culture. Not only is that socially and culturally inescapable; it is also theologically demanded when the worship of God and the God who is worshiped are understood incarnationally. It is not a negation of the congregation's "Christianness" but a function of its "Christianness."

On the other hand, each instance of the congregation's ideological bondage clearly is an instance of faithlessness to its identity, a faithlessness in both the adoration of God and works of love.

Insofar as human interests are indifferent to or incommensurate with the interests central to God's mission in Jesus, ideological bondage in the broad sense distorts the patterns of conduct, outlook, and story in which a congregation adores God. And insofar as it is rooted in interests contradicting God's mission in Jesus, ideological bondage in the narrow sense distorts those patterns even more. Either way, these distortions are serious. For it is largely by means of participation in the various activities that comprise the adoration of God that the personal identities of a congregation's members are evoked, nurtured, and corrected as identities characterized by faith, hope, and love. Thus when the patterns of these activities are distorted, the personal identities will likewise be changed.

A congregation's works of love can also be distorted by its ideological bondage, particularly in its narrow sense. Christian works of love, as responses to the biblical stories of God's mission in Jesus, should help remove social injustice. But it is precisely such action that is subverted when a congregation's patterns of conduct and outlook are tied to the interests of that population that benefits from such injustice. The communal self-reflection that is necessary to a faithful response to the biblical stories about God's mission in Jesus (that is, the self-reflection that is essential to a congregation's adoration of God) is what is negated by its ideological bondage in the narrow sense.

What are the implications of this for the proposal that the study of the congregation be a focus for theological education? The ideological bias of Christian congregations should not be used as a criterion of exclusion as a focus for theological education. Rather, the principle of exclusion might be this: Any group that worships God in Jesus' name but that contains no voices calling for the correction of its ideological biases should be excluded as not Christian, despite its avowal of "Jesus' name." The principle of inclusion should be "Christianness," not "sinlessness." Thus not even congregations that are ideological in the narrow sense should be excluded. Instead, congregations whose social location gives them the interests of those victimized by social injustices should be studied along with congregations ideologically bound in the narrow sense. And both should be compared with those few congregations whose social location places them among the beneficiaries of their society's political and economic power arrangements but who are struggling to find ways to relocate themselves politically. Study of the congregation can serve as the centerpiece of a reformed theological education only if several different congregations together are its focus.

The Congregation Catholic

The third problem about making study of the congregation central to theological education is that it may imply a schismatic and sectarian view of the church. On one side, concentrating on the congregation may split the congregations being studied from the great church ecumenical. On the other side, the same concentration may separate the congregation from its greater social context, as though a sectarian understanding of the church were normative. But I think that my suggestions regarding the concept of congregation show that making study of the congregation a focus of theological education need not have these consequences.

The conceptual task here is to indicate how the concepts of church and congregation are related to each other. Several temptations should be resisted. One is to suggest that the church's invisible reality is marked by its permanence and that individual congregations are best thought of as diverse and relatively impermanent manifestations, "events," or "acts" of the church. That temptation should be resisted on the grounds that the congregation is to be understood as an enduring reality with a concrete location in physical and social space. The congregation cannot be adequately understood in the rhetoric of events alone. A second temptation is to suggest that the "church" is an abstract ideal of which congregations are particulars, concrete and relatively enduring instantiations. That temptation is to be resisted on the grounds that the great church is as concretely actual as is any congregation. The relation between church and congregation cannot be adequately understood in the rhetoric of ideal possibility and concrete actualization. A third temptation is to suggest that the great church and the local congregation are related as are a great commercial corporation and its several outlets (as the Great Atlantic and Pacific Tea Company is to our local A & P). This suggestion does preserve the concreteness of both church and congregation. But it is to be resisted because it implies that just as no particular outlet of the A & P is more than a small part of a greater whole, so no individual congregation is, or has, more than a part of the church's reality. But although in practice every congregation in its sinful faithlessness lacks something of the church's fullness, there is no reason that if it were fully faithful, each congregation could not have the fullness of the church.

These three temptations together suggest that as a conceptual point it is better to speak of a "local" congregation than of a "particular" congregation. We have already seen that a congregation has a specific location. "Particular," however, may imply a momentary appearance of an underlying reality, a concrete particularization of an abstract ideal, or a particular part (the branch office) of a complex whole (the central bank). But a congregation is not the particularization of anything; it is the church local.

Perhaps we can avoid these temptations by understanding the relation between the great church and the congregation in terms of worship. All congregations are groups of persons gathered to celebrate, in Hopewell's phrase, "a more universally practiced" worship. It is the same worship that is universally practiced by all Christian congregations because it is, despite its variations, a response to the same thing: the stories of Jesus' mission and God's mission in Jesus. These stories, furthermore, provide all celebrations of Christian worship with basically the same lexicon of symbols, images, metaphors, and parables. And because they all are responses to the same stories, culturally diverse celebrations of Christian worship are basically similar. One consequence of this is that the communal identities of Christian congregations and the personal identities of their members have family resemblances despite the differences among them. A second consequence is that the life of all Christian congregations has the same mission in patterns of conduct, outlook, and story that are faithful to the mission of Jesus. The same images and parables, identity, and mission make up the reality of the great church. Thus the church is always localize*able* but never locali*zed*. It can never be localized because no one social or geographic locus can define it. But it is always localizeable in that the adoration of God and works of love for neighbor that comprise its reality consist of temporally extended actions that must, by definition, have both a physical and social location. Every such localization is a congregation. Consequently, a study of the congregation would necessarily resist both a schism of individual congregations from the "church catholic" and a sectarian separation of congregations from their social locations. Indeed, it would require a study of the congregation carried out in the context of a global consciousness of the great church and its protean acculturations.

This requires one final modification of our answer to the question, What counts as a Christian congregation? Our fifth answer is

1. A Christian congregation is a group of persons that gathers together to celebrate a universally practiced worship of God.

2. This group explicitly does so "in Jesus' name" as a deliberate act of self-identification.

3. This group does so regularly enough for an indefinite period of time to have a common life in which develop intrinsic patterns of conduct, outlook, and story.

4. This group holds its conduct, outlook, and story accountable as to its faithfulness to biblical stories of Jesus' mission and God's mission in Jesus.

MINISTRY TO THE WORLD: A NEW PROFESSIONAL PARADIGM

John B. Cobb, Jr.

There is an obvious truth in the proposal that theological education should take the congregation seriously. Its primary purpose is to prepare leadership for congregations. When this point is made, most of us immediately recognize that we have neglected it. This is more true of those of us in the so-called classical disciplines, but even professors of pastoral theology tend to view the congregation chiefly or entirely from the perspective of the minister. Thus the seminary contributes to clericalism.

Clericalism has been a problem throughout the history of Christianity. From time to time it seems that some segment of the church has disposed of it and truly become a community of believers. But what begin as lay movements usually end as clericized as any others are.

This has certainly been true of my own denomination. Methodism began as a movement of lay preaching and the self-organization of lay people. Later the preachers were ordained, but their function in this country was to spread the movement on the frontier. The settled congregations were largely led by laypersons. Gradually the clergy took over the settled congregations. The annual conferences that had initially functioned to allow the settled congregations to work in mission have become clergy associations to ensure job security and pensions.

We must recognize that this change has accompanied higher requirements for education and increasing support for seminaries. The seminaries are a part of this clerical dominance. Whether we have actively promoted it or been unwitting tools, I do not know, but clearly we have offered little protest.

The situation has grown worse in my denomination as it declines in membership and resources. Fifty years ago it was still possible to understand being a Methodist as being part of a movement in mission. Such a movement could expect some sacrifices from both its laity and its clergy. But as it declines, attention shifts from mission to maintenance. A reasonably paid clergy becomes the top priority in the allocation of funds. Other spending is adjusted accordingly.

As a member of my denomination's commission on its mission, I have been impressed by the intensity of the revulsion against this situation felt by bishops, ministers, and lay people. Many feel that we simply cannot get on with the mission of the church unless this clericalism is overcome. My view is that we cannot break the power of clericalism unless we become clear about our mission and rededicated to it. In either case, there are implications for theological education.

Hopewell criticized the clergy paradigm of theological education. There is clear resonance between his criticism and the concern I am expressing here about the connection of theological education and clericalism. But I continue to have difficulty understanding what else theological education can have as its primary task than the preparation of clergy for the churches. I would favor a massive movement of lay education, but that would not be a reform of theological education. It would be something quite new. I think instead that what is important is that theological education try to prepare leaders for the church who will genuinely understand themselves as servants of the church.

It will also be important that we help these future leaders think carefully about the nature of the church they will serve. In some denominations it may be appropriate to identify this church with congregations. In my case it is not. In Methodist history, congregations have also been servants of the church, trying to organize their lives so as to advance a mission they share with one another and that is carried out through noncongregational structures. I believe that to some extent this is true of all the denominations we represent. In any case, my view is that a congregation that seeks in its leaders only those who will serve its felt needs is as bad as clergy who view the laity chiefly as a source of assuring them a good career and a secure retirement.

I have tried to indicate why I think this project could be fruitful as a check on rampant clericalism and also why I find it misdirected. I believe it pointless to oppose the clerical paradigm of theological education if by that we mean that theological education is primarily engaged in preparing clergy. I fear that the focus on the congregation can encourage the ingrownness of the church that is already its basic disease. Because the problem of clericalism is real and important, and one that the church will have difficulty addressing without some help and even leadership from the theological schools, I shall offer some comments on what I see as possible.

At one time I thought the problem was the professionalization of the ministry. My impression was that as the clergy insisted that they were professionals, they increasingly emphasized their prerogatives and status. They compared themselves with other professionals and complained that they were not accorded equal compensation for their services.

On the other hand, the status of the ministry as a profession is an ancient and honorable one. And to be professional means also to have high standards for one's work and one's conduct. It entails holding other members of the profession accountable to those standards. All this seemed healthy.

I gradually learned, with the guidance of Joseph Hough, that the distaste

I felt for professionalism was a reaction to a form of professionalism that developed in the nineteenth century. This was connected with the duality of theory and practice. It encouraged a hierarchical view in which the highest status was awarded to the theoreticians and the second rank to those who mediated between theory and practice. The latter was the professional class. The professionals knew less theory than the theoreticians did and were not engaged in advancing theoretical knowledge. But they did share in theoretical knowledge in ways that separated them from those they served, and they knew how to apply that knowledge to practical problems.

The engineer was a good example of the new professional. Engineers were well educated in some branch of physics or chemistry, but they did not become physicists or chemists. They learned enough so that they could apply relevant aspects of modern science to practical problems.

Of the ancient professions, medicine could adapt best to the new situation. Doctors learned a great deal about the biological sciences and the chemical properties of drugs. But they did not become scientists. Instead, their special function was to apply this theoretical knowledge gained by research scientists to the problems of the human body.

This view of professionals attributes to them a knowledge not available to those they serve. They are the experts whose authoritative answers to the problems of the rest of us are simply to be accepted and followed. We are grateful if they condescend to explain in lay terms the reasons for their recommendations, but chiefly we pay them to solve our problems and not to explain them to us. Neither law nor Christian ministry can fit this model comfortably, but there is a strong if subtle tendency to adapt in that direction. Lawyers cannot apply a science to practical problems, but they can view their superior knowledge of law and the legal system in a similar way. If one goes to a lawyer for advice, one may have the situation explained. But there is also a sense that the lawyer is the one who knows and that one should follow legal advice whether or not one understands its rationale.

If to be a professional is to have access to an esoteric lore that enables one to solve the problems of those who do not share the knowledge, then what about the ministry? Can it be a profession? Theological schools have given some color to the claim that it is, by distinguishing theoretical and practical disciplines. The implication of this language is that there is a theory that can guide practice. The increasing requirements for the education of ministers have increased the gap between the minister's knowledge of scripture, of church history, and of theology and that of lay people generally. Hence this knowledge can be viewed as the esoteric theory on the basis of which the minister can function as an expert in relation to the church's practical needs.

One does not have to examine the situation very closely to see that this has not worked. The minister's esoteric knowledge of the Bible, church history, and theology provides her or him with little guidance in giving leadership to the church. It may influence preaching, but even there its role is surprisingly modest, despite the best efforts of seminary faculties. Even within seminary education itself, it is clear that those who teach in the "practical" disciplines do not apply to the problems of the church what is learned in the "theoretical" disciplines. If they apply theoretical disciplines at all, these are found much more in the social sciences, sciences that still play a very small role in the theological curriculum.

For theological schools to encourage ministers to think of themselves as professionals in this modern sense is unwarranted, and the effort to play the professional role leads to inauthenticity. It has seriously damaged the Christian ministry. If this is what it means to be a professional, then seminaries should join with others in the church in attacking the professionalization of the ministry.

I have been persuaded to forgo an attack on professionalization only by my realization that other models of the professional are emerging. Students and leaders of other professions are also recognizing that the application of theory to the solution of problems is a limited and unsatisfactory definition. It is challenged even in medicine where it has worked the best. Indeed, there is a widespread revolt against a system of medicine in which increasingly narrow expertise is applied to increasingly limited features of the body. Rather, there is a growing recognition of the interconnectedness of all parts of the body and of the body with the psyche. The informed participation of the patient in the treatment is also acknowledged as important. Adequate health care requires that people be well informed about what makes for health and be empowered to care for themselves.

Of course, this does not mean that the specialized knowledge of some has ceased to be important. But it fits into a wider context. The professional here can be seen as one who works with patients in the inclusive attention to their health. Experience with other patients becomes as important as scientific knowledge in informing this approach. The specialized skills of experts in particular aspects of the body and in technical procedures will be used as the professional and the patients together come to see the need for such help. This is the model of the professional as a reflective practitioner.[1]

The empowering of the patient should not be understood as simply midwifery. Truly to empower is to share knowledge and experience and to make proposals. It is to envision and inspire, to encourage and guide. Professionals need to lead in the fullest sense. They are not mere catalysts.

If we can think of professionals in this sense, then we can enthusiastically reaffirm that Christian ministry is a profession. It has been such a profession all along. But to be such a profession is to reject clericalism. The profession exists for the service of the church, and that means for the empowerment of

---

[1] See Donald Schön, *The Reflective Practitioner: How Professionals Think in Action* (New York: Basic Books, 1983).

the church. The church that is empowered cannot be primarily the professional leadership!

To empower the church includes, centrally, empowering congregations for participation in the mission of the church. The seminary can help prepare ministers for that role. To do so it must attend to the congregation, in both its actuality and its potentiality.

Some of the attention to the congregation can be detached and scientific. But for the most part the attention will be guided by normative questions that are not likely to arise from scientific inquiry. The question is, In what ways are congregations fulfilling their Christian calling? How can they change so as to fulfill this calling better? What role can leadership play in the reform and renewal of congregational life? How can Christian lay people truly be empowered to be more fully Christian individually and collectively?

Seminaries certainly have the responsibility to help future ministers ask these questions, but their contribution here will always be minimal. Every congregation is different, and there is no way that seminary graduates can gain an adequate understanding of congregations by studying them in academic courses. Coming to understand congregations is a part of the lifetime work of reflective practitioners. Those best qualified to help will be other reflective practitioners already long experienced.

Most ministers, as they mature, do learn how to "size up" congregations quite insightfully. At this they are far more adept than are professors in schools of theology. Formal education can help by introducing students to some of the tools available to refine common sense, but reflective practice guided by experienced reflective practitioners is primary.

The principal responsibility of academic theological education lies elsewhere. When ministers size up congregations, from what perspective do they do so? Often it has to do with structures of power and potential for growth. These are proper concerns. But too rarely do they size them up from the point of view of the potential of more adequately responding to God's call.

This is partly because there is insufficient clarity and conviction with respect to what God calls the church to be and to do. It is here that the major responsibility of the seminary lies. The normative questions are the ones to which we should be giving the greatest attention. Our teaching of Bible, church history, and theology should be normative through and through. This is not theory in relation to practice. But it is the shaping of a perspective from which the whole task of the church and its ministry is to be viewed.

This can be done only through the study of Bible, church history, and theology. But it cannot be done through this study alone. Too often the normative thinking that comes out of these classrooms is so disconnected with the actual life of congregations that it serves only to trouble ministers, not to guide them in their professional work. Seminary is not the place for learning how practically to solve this problem in individual instances. But it must take as its responsibility helping to think through the relation of Christian ideals and norms to the real church. It should help fashion an understanding of the minister's work that is informed by ideals and norms that do in fact relate helpfully to daily tasks.

Such an education can help prepare men and women for a lifetime of learning as reflective practitioners who always understand their reflective practice as service to the church. This is different from the situation of reflective practitioners in other professions. Insofar as they are normatively oriented, their norms will be personal ones, or those of their clients, or those of the wider society. In the long run it will be disastrous for the church if reflective practice of ministry works in this way. The norms governing such practice will work against the healthy continuance of the church if they are not the norms of the church.

If I am correct, then the central concern of theological education will be normative. That these norms need to be shaped in real relation to congregations I have tried to emphasize. But they are not to be derived primarily from study of individual congregations. They are derived from study of what the individual congregations publicly acknowledge to be their norms. The seminary is particularly well qualified to study those norms and to interpret them. It should do this task well.

Thus far I have ignored questions that are, for me, more important than the ones on which I have touched. I have dealt with the nature of leadership in the congregation and how theological education is related to that. But we could work quite effectively along these lines while the world rushed on to self-destruction. A few of the congregations we study might raise for us the urgent questions of nuclear war, ecological collapse, and overwhelming social oppression and repression, but the greater likelihood is that these topics would be peripheral. In my opinion, to treat these as peripheral would be disastrous.

My counterproposal is not that we should ignore congregations but that we should focus more on the world than on the church. Norms for congregations and for ministry in congregations should come out of judgments about God's mission in the world. Because congregational life and ministry within congregations are so important to those whom we educate, we may certainly speak of them as *a* focus of theological education! But I can only say that after I have first identified the primary foci in another way.

My failure to raise this point before this late place in my paper itself illustrates the danger of the focus on the congregation. Identifying the congregation as the focus led me, in response, to restrict my attention to narrowly ecclesiological questions. The world did not function even as a horizon for viewing these questions. David Kelsey's paper almost persuades me that there is a slight possibility that a curriculum focusing on the congregation can avoid this narrowness. But I do not see any reason to adopt a curriculum whose overwhelming tendency would be to marginalize the most important problems faced by all of us, including the congregations.

Allow me to summarize my conclusions. First, it makes no sense to me to shift from a clergy paradigm to a congregational one in theological education. Our task will continue to be to educate clergy and other leaders for the congregation.

Second, we should rid ourselves of every vestige of the theory-practice view of theological education. This is related to an image of the minister as a particular kind of professional that the church should always have rejected. This image has encouraged the clericalism we should work against.

Third, we need an image of the minister as a reflective practitioner that will show what the seminary can do to help prepare ministers and also the important role of experienced ministers. Our emphasis can be that the minister's task is to empower the congregation to fulfill its mission. This will work against clericalism.

Fourth, our primary task is to clarify normatively what it means to be a church. It is my assumption that this will entail showing that both the congregations and the ministers should order their lives to ends that lie far beyond their personal and institutional goals. This too would work against clericalism.

Fifth, for the church to be the church today is for it to serve God's mission in the world. To be a leader in the church is to understand the world to which we all are sent. Any focus on the church should be in the context of attention to the world and God's mission in it.

WHICH CONGREGATIONS?
A MISSION FOCUS FOR THEOLOGICAL EDUCATION

Letty M. Russell

Which congregation is James Hopewell talking about in "A Congregational Paradigm for Theological Education"? David Kelsey helped identify which congregation in his paper, and I basically agree with his understanding. I would describe a Christian congregation as people gathered in the name of Jesus Christ, who often discover in their midst the gifts of *kerygma*, *koinonia*, *diakonia*, and *leiturgia*. Matthew 18:20 seems to indicate that the center of a Christian community is the person and presence of Christ, who promises to be with the people wherever they gather to call on Christ's name.

But it seems to me that the meaning of Christian congregation (even if it is expanded) is not broad or diverse enough to encompass what students study in theological schools or how we should design courses of theological education. Among the problems that the shift from a clerical to a congregational paradigm does not show are nationalism, racism, classism, heterosexism, sexism, and guildism. Despite all the clarifications, the assumed congregational model still looks like the largely white, male-dominated, middle-class, Protestant church that David Kelsey attends in Branford. In fact, it looks a great deal like the seminaries from which we come and also like most of us, because we would be choosing the congregations. If so, it is not likely to provide a fresh, pluralistic alternative, let alone the subversion for which Hopewell calls. Underlying the choice of congregational models are who chooses them and whose questions they will help answer.

With these questions in mind and with some attention to a more fundamental one, why should we even consider a congregational paradigm? I shall examine the Hopewell and Kelsey Proposals and then indicate an alternative direction that these discussions might take.

Before I begin, however, I want to clarify my perspective. I am not against congregations; I care about them, and I worked in a parish as both educator and pastor for seventeen years. I know that people in parishes have many gifts and manage to teach much to their pastors, church workers, officers, and seminary-student interns. They would also have much to teach seminary professors if those professors wanted to listen.

I also agree that the relationship of theological education to the congregations needs to be thought through and that the congregational paradigm is helpful in addressing two important problems in our seminaries, churches, and culture: the dualisms of thought and action, mind and body spelled out in Marjorie Suchocki's paper, as well as the individualist model of autonomous professional, or mental health, practitioner.

Many people have pointed to the bankruptcy of these clerical models of education, and the congregational focus seems to be a good way to transcend the dualism of school and church. But it does keep the basic clerical paradigm at the heart of the congregation. The congregations' record regarding these dualisms is not very good, and so there may be a catch here in the concreteness of congregational life.

Which Christian Congregations?

One of Kelsey's questions seems to me to be key to our discussion. He asks, "Is it really possible to invoke the congregation as a focus for theological education without also giving pride of place to an ideologically distorted load of meaning one would wish rather to denounce?" When reading Kelsey's development of this question, I thought of the old television program "To Tell the Truth." Some of you may remember that the different guests would tell their occupational stories; someone would guess who the real "plumber," "bartender," or "shoplifter" was; and the real one would stand up and be identified. Likewise, in order to use the congregational paradigm, we have to tell the stories of many congregations and then ask the real congregation to stand up! I agree with Kelsey about the importance and attractiveness of dealing with the congregation in the concrete, and I would underline the problems he identified in this concreteness: cultural differences among churches, ideological captivity, and possible sectarianism or lack of global perspective.

Kelsey answered the first problem by naming the center of congregational life as that of worship and self-identification with Christ and Jesus' mission in a way that transcends cultural barriers. He then stressed the importance of varieties of congregations as a corrective to ideological captivity and described the local congregation as an expression of the whole, catholic church. I want to suggest ways that these problems might also be addressed from the perspective of a mission paradigm, but first I want to look at the problems of the congregational paradigm itself.

From my perspective, the answer to Kelsey's question is that it is not possible to invoke the congregation as a focus for theological education without also implying pride of place. I say this because a plan probably will not succeed that puts even more pressure on what is generally a weaker area of theological education (or at least a less prestigious area among the guilds), that of pastoral education. It also is not likely to convert those who look down on pastoral theology and are interested only in their academic disciplines, or to provide the institutional support needed for such a change.

If the congregational paradigm were implemented in some way, those marginal to the seminary and to most congregations might be in an even worse position. The authors of *God's Fierce Whimsy* described theological education as "in some fundamental ways, a bad experience for women and men of all colors and cultures who seek primarily to know and love a God of justice."[1] For women, working in congregations is often more difficult than is participating in seminary life. Indeed, seminary life usually is pleasant and thus hides from women the difficulties they will face in congregations. In addition, there are fewer and fewer jobs for women graduates in congregations, even for those trained to serve in congregations.

In some settings, however, the congregational paradigm might work very well. I do not want to rule out its appropriateness to certain contexts, especially those linked to denominational structures. As indicated by the small urban program taught by Ardith Hayes at Union Theological Seminary, it is also possible to use the congregational paradigm as part of a more diverse seminary program. But I do think that a mission paradigm might be one on which we should concentrate.

God's Mission

In 1969 I wrote in my doctoral thesis at Union Theological Seminary[2] that mission, not ministry, is the key to understanding new possibilities for theological education, and since then I have not changed my mind. First, the focus on ministry and the minister has many problems with which we are familiar. For instance, when we move beyond the consensus that there is one ministry, that of Jesus Christ, into which we all are baptized as Christians, we find that there is little consensus on ministry inside or outside the congregations. Even the World Council of Churches convergence document on baptism, eucharist, and ministry is really an agreement to disagree over many matters crucial to the ministry, including the ordination of women. Second, we are frustrated in training for the ministry because we do not know for which congregations we are training. Actual training in pastoral and prophetic ministry is usually a matter of playing catch-up: "This is how I used to do it, but you will have to do it in many different ways in the future." Third, the continuation of the clergy-laity split seriously undermines any claims to a genuinely congregational ministry.

An important alternative paradigm for theological education is God's mission. In my view, we as educators are participating in God's trinitarian

---

[1] The Mud Flower Collective, *God's Fierce Whimsy* (New York: Pilgrim Press, 1985), 32.

[2] Letty Russell, "Tradition As Mission: Study of a New Current in Theology and Its Implications for Theological Education" (Ph.D. diss., Union Theological Seminary, 1969).

sending and traditioning activity, and the goal of theological education is continuing participation in that activity. The concept of *missio Dei* has been understood in theology as God's sending, traditioning, and liberating work through Jesus Christ. In this sense the church does not have a mission, but rather, it participates in God's mission in the redemption of humanity and the restoration of all creation. God's economic activity continues in the work of housekeeping and invites us all to take part through acts of justice and shalom.

When we look at this from the eschatological perspective of Luke's story of Jesus' ministry, we discover that the focus of all our forms of ministry, including theological education, is on reaching out to those who are marginal, poor, and outcast from society and making them welcome in God's household (Luke 4:18-19). We educate ourselves for those whom God is seeking to include as members of his creation. In a mission paradigm the focus is not, as in Kelsey's paper, *ecclesiocentric* (God/church/world) but, rather, *oikocentric* (God/world/church). Theological education should begin with the mission and the needs of the world. This is not a one-sided appeal to social action but an appeal to the God's own *oikonomia*.

Theological Education and God's Mission

In *The Liberation of Theology*, Juan Luis Segundo stated that prior political commitment to the poor creates a way of experiencing reality that is the first step in the hermeneutical circle.[3] Likewise, when designing studies of theological education, to begin with God's mission is to make a similar commitment that becomes a first step in creating an alternative paradigm. This prior commitment to participate in God's housekeeping activity in the world determines how we will interpret scripture and tradition and how we will value methods of investigation. Theological education is seen through the experience of those engaged in God's mission, communities of struggle for justice and shalom, inside and outside traditional congregational structures. Some familiar examples of this are the basic Christian communities, women-churches, sanctuary churches, and churches of people of color. They provide knowledge of oppressive structures and point us to questions that may indicate what God's missionary action on behalf of all creation really is.

In the light of God's mission, we still must deal with the problems that Kelsey outlined, but the perspective shifts. God's mission does not come third, after worship and self-identification with Jesus, as Kelsey seems to imply. Rather, it becomes the way along which worship and identity occur. The life-style of Jesus, *diakonia*, is not a form of practical application but is the passport description of what it means to follow, whether in seminary, in church, or in some other group committed to minding creation. Ideological

[3] Juan Luis Segundo, *The Liberation of Theology* (Maryknoll, N.Y.: Orbis Books, 1976), 9.

captivity is challenged not only with pluralism but also with the claim that the community of faith must be joined by the community of struggle in interpreting the meaning of the gospel message and in setting the theological agenda. Learning needs to take place in both the disarray of the world and in communities struggling to overcome that disarray on behalf of the "excluded ones." And the concrete signs of God's housekeeping work appear in many places within and beyond the congregation and seminary.

Such a mission paradigm is risky because it is open-ended and also open to the whole human race. But its very openness is important because it prevents us from straightening the curriculum by excluding from it all those who do not fit. Instad, it sets a course toward God's intended future and invites all of us to come along in working to transform the present by creating anticipatory signs of God's justice and shalom, inside as well as outside the seminary.

This paradigm is obviously eschatological, and yet it is concrete. We often do know when God's will is done on earth as in heaven; when the lame walk and the blind see and the poor have good news preached to them (Matt. 11:2-6). This is what we celebrate in the biblical story, in our own stories, and in our worship. Perhaps mission would provide the focus for a more constructive curriculum. So "let us run with perseverance the race that is set before us," together with all those who care about the disarray of our groaning and hoping world (Heb. 12:1-2).

A THEOLOGICAL CURRICULUM ABOUT AND AGAINST THE CHURCH

David H. Kelsey

Why would a theological school want to revise its curriculum? The urge to do so seems to come over some of us in theological education with an almost seasonal regularity. Indeed, I have helped design and lobby for at least four different curricular revisions. As I look back on those efforts, most of which did not lead to proposals that were adopted, it seems clear that for some of us, there are two different reasons for wanting curricular reform.

First, we may believe that the educational process is not working as well as it ought to. We may also assume that we know the goals of the process and so need to revise the means to achieve them, an assumption that is not always warranted. Sometimes there is solid or highly suggestive evidence that the process is valid. But I shall have to leave this concern to others. I am not an educational theorist and cannot add much to discussions about the best means to achieve a seminary's educational goals.

The other reason for reform is theological: We believe that no matter how sound it is by other standards, the curriculum is theologically inadequate. Because I am a theologian and have formed some opinions about these matters, I welcome the opportunity to reflect on that judgment and its possible implications for a more adequate curriculum.

The Idea of Curriculum

"Curriculum" is a metaphor. Literally, a curriculum is a running course. Used metaphorically in regard to education, it is, or ought to be, a unified course of study. In our culture, a curriculum is conventionally divided into discrete units, called *courses*. Ideally, each course has some sort of internal integrity that enables us to quantify the educational process by ascribing basic value units, or credits, to each course. A particular number of course credits is a quantifiable criterion in determining whether a degree will be earned at the end of a course of study. No one of these courses is itself the course of study. But at the same time (and this is important), a theological school's curriculum should provide a course of study, not a clutch of courses.

How is a curriculum integrated into a course of study? In large part, its constituent elements (for example, the courses that comprise the curriculum) should seek common ends. There is a conventional widsom, though not a consensus, about this among theological educators. There are two different views regarding the ends that the curriculum of a theological school should address, and so there are two different ways in which the curriculum's adequacy may be assessed on theological grounds.

These views are widespread, according to a review of the past three years of the Association of Theological Schools' Issues Research Program. The following pattern emerged both in the assumptions of research projects that theological educators proposed for the program's funding and in the thirteen issues that the program's binational conference of theological educators voted as the most important issues confronting theological education for the balance of the century.[1]

In one way, every subject in a theological school's curriculum should be taught and learned so that it elucidates the Christian faith. In another way every subject in a theololgical curriculum should be taught so that it addresses the practice of the ministry in a pluralistic world. Accordingly, the curriculum may be inadequate because it does not teach an ideal unity of the faith. Or it may be inadequate because it does not address the real pluralism of the ministry's worlds. In any case, this is the conventional wisdom.

Both kinds of theological assessment of curricula focus on the individual theological student. According to the first assessment, a curriculum will be a genuine course of study if its primary aim is to elucidate "the faith" for the student. When the faith is interpreted more intellectually, the curriculum will be more logical, as though what is taught first, say scripture and the history of doctrine, has the logical status of first principles on which all that is taught later logically depends either directly or through the mediation of middle principles. Here the faith is accessible and can be adequately stated. If properly learned, it will structure the student's mind and life. But when the faith is construed in a more actualist or existentialist way (as it is in neoorthodox or dialectical circles), the curriculum can be less rigid. Through the diversity of the curriculum's subjects, the event of The Word or The Kerygma or The Tradition will be introduced into the student's life. When the faith is construed in a third way, as a mode of preconceptual consciousness, the curriculum will be a course of study insofar as it helps form that consciousness in the student and enables its expression. In the latter two cases, the faith—the proper subject matter of a theological curriculum lying behind all of the curriculum's various courses—is itself elusive. Consequently, the faith is difficult to use either as the criterion by which to establish that the curriculum is fragmented or as the focal point that could reunite it. According to all three views of the faith, the curriculum is an integral whole, despite its diversity of disciplines and subjects and its tem-

[1] See David H. Kelsey and Barbara G. Wheeler, "Mind-Reading: Notes on the Basic Issues Program," *Theological Education* 20 (Spring 1984): 8–14.

poral extension, because it shapes the individual student, that is, the student's mind or existence or prethematized consciousness.

This same individualistic focus is implicit in theological judgments that the conventional theological curriculum is inadequate because it is ideologically captive to one social world and inappropriate to the plurality of the other worlds in which ministry must be executed. In this case, the curriculum would be judged to be a course of study if it addressed the practice of ministry informed by the pluralism of those worlds in which it must be practiced. Such a curriculum would expose the students to other social worlds than the ones they have taken for granted. The students would then become acquainted with the diverse conditions imposed by the pluralism of the ministry's worlds. The students would also have to confront their own ideological assumptions that the styles of ministry with which they are familiar are identical with Christian ministry. This assessment of the theological curriculum also assumes that a curriculum adequate to the contextual pluralism of Christian ministry focuses on the individual student.

I shall sketch an alternative, nonindividualistic picture of the ends to which all subjects could be taught and studies in the theological curriculum so as to make the curriculum a course of study and not a clutch of courses. I will not argue against the individualistic point of view assumed by the conventional wisdom about what is wrong with theological curricula; I take for granted a consensus that there are very strong theological objections to that sort of individualism. Before turning in that direction, however, I think it is important to put this entire discussion of specifically curricular reform within very emphatic brackets.

It is important not only to acknowledge but also to stress how little a reformed curriculum is likely to change the quality of a seminary's educational program. It does not matter how radical the reform is. A new curriculum by itself would not be able to overcome the countervailing power of the seminary's two other elements, its faculty and its traditional ethos. The faculty's potentialities for change in the educational process are defined by its actuality and not by the ideal possibilities for change sketched by a new curriculum. Second, by an ethos, I mean the institution's culture that it transmits from generation to generation. This culture is a mixture of power relationships, patterns of behavior, and shared attitudes and dispositions. It shapes and limits education, and it is as resistant to change as it is difficult to analyze. Reform of the curriculum, that is, of the structure of courses that may become a course of study, is unlikely to alter this culture, or ethos, as much as the ethos is likely to absorb the reformed curriculum.

I want to suggest that the aim of theological education is to teach persons to be learned pastors, and the curriculum that does this best is one that concentrates on the communal identity of particular Christian churches, what that identity is, how it is called into being and nurtured, and how it is corrected and reformed. The phrase "learned pastor" sounds, I know, down-

right quaint. It elicits a large choir of stereotyped reactions. I hope to
neutralize the inconclusive debates the stereotypes generate by giving the
notion a new twist.

About and Against the Church

One of my colleagues insists that our theological school is now more like
an upper-level catechetical school than like any of the traditional models for
theological schools. This description fits not only university-related divinity
schools but also many denominational seminaries. The change has nothing to
do with the proportion of graduates who take ordained or church-related
positions, compared with the proportion who remain lay people. Rather, this
change means that a theological course of studies pertains more to persons'
growing into a Christian identity than their growing into the role of a
professional churchperson. No longer can the theological school's curriculum
assume that most of the students, having been socialized into the church at
an early age, are familiar with the rudiments of the church and now need
only to be introduced to a specialized role within the larger community of
faith. Instead, students begin this curriculum when they already have developed their career-role identities and are moving into an identification with
the Christian community as adults without having had earlier significant
church involvement. Indeed, the role of a theological school today may be
closer to that of the Christian academy that Origen operated in third-century
pagan Alexandria than it is to the role of any educational venture in Christendom since then. I suspect that my colleague takes this change to be a sign of
terrible decline, but I want to suggest the opposite, that it provides a social
and cultural foundation for improvement in theological education. I believe
that the curriculum should be redesigned as a genuine course of studies by
addressing the end to which the current curriculum is being skewed anyway:
the nature and nurture of the communal identity of Christian faith. Let it
become a curriculum *about* the church and a curriculum *against* the church.

Every local church is a concretely actual community with a communal
identity. Stress needs to fall on its *concrete* actuality. Innovative ecclesiologies in the 1960s and 1970s tended to describe the church in a rhetoric
of "event." The church was something that "happened." Between such
"happenings," all one had was an objectivizing institution. But this rhetoric
has little connection to that community of which I am a part and that meets
in a white building on the Green in Branford, Connecticut. That is the
concrete reality of a church, and it is the one concrete datum we have
available to work with in theological education.

Theological education must focus on the communal identity of Christian
communities, and identities, communal as well as individual, are best expressed in narratives. Local churches use two different kinds of narrative to
explain who they are. They can tell stories about their local history, the

important turning points in their common life, their roles in the community and its culture, their relations with other local congregations and their denomination, and their prospects for the future. These stories then become part of larger stories about the larger communities whose culture is to the church a kind of host culture. Communities also explain who they are by using biblical narratives to describe their identity. It needs to be stressed that these are stories, plural not singular. Church communities establish their identity by means of sermons, the use of scripture in religious education, and the structure of their services of worship, particularly of the sacraments of baptism and eucharist.

Both the nonbiblical and the biblical stories are usually told in the first person plural ("We are the people who . . ."), although stories may also be told in the third person plural, from the perspective of an observer rather than a participant ("They are people who . . ."). Both the nonbiblical and biblical stories told in the first person plural concern the same concrete reality: a particular congregation of Christians. It is a mistake to suppose that each story has a different referent, one, say, to the reality of the church and the other to its appearance, one to something inner, perhaps subjective, unavailable to observation and authentic, and the other to something outer, objectivized, observable, and inauthentic. Rather, their common referent is a complex and open system of embodied human action that can be located and observed in time and space. It is also a mistake to suppose that one of the two can be subordinated, or reduced to, the other. Nor can they be subsumed in some third embracing and synthesizing superstory. There is no systematic interrelating of the two kinds of narrative; an adequate account of the church must rest on the identifying descriptions provided by both kinds of stories. Perhaps that is why, along with the Incarnation and the human person, the church in classical theology has been called a mystery: In all three cases, though for different reasons, Christians struggle to describe an identity that may be rendered only through two different kinds of narrative that cannot either be reduced one to the other or systematically interrelated.

My proposal stresses the study of the communal identities of particular congregations of Christians and so raises two questions. The first is whether the proposal favors a "congregationalist" ecclesiology over a more catholic and "connectional" understanding of the church. The second concerns the criteria by which a community is deemed a genuinely "Christian" community. The answer to the first is no. Most ecclesiologies include two themes: that God's church is, theologically, one ecumenical reality (or "the" church) and that the church's full reality is present in each particular place (or "a" church). The theological differences among the several Christian communions are, generally, differences within these two themes. The second of these themes permits a focus on the communal identities of particular local congregations. Because the full reality of "the church" is present in each congregation, part of its identity is the sense that it is one with the worldwide people of God. But the specific way in which that aspect of communal identity is sensed will differ according to the way in which the congregation identifies itself by means of biblical narratives and nonbiblical local histories. That is, particular congregation's nonbiblical histories of themselves will include stories about their relationships with other local congregations and with "the church" nationally and globally.

The criteria by which a community is deemed a Christian community can be left general: The community understands itself as called into being by God's grace, particularly in Jesus of Nazareth; it sees its common life to be a communal response to God's grace; central to that response is acts of praise to God; and in the community's common life. biblical writings are used to shape its identity and those of its members.[2] These criteria do not apply to any one systematic ecclesiology. In practice, the range and diversity of the churches that a theological school could study would be limited by, for example, the school's denominationally defined mission, its theological understanding of itself, and the degree of religious pluralism in the school's geographical location.

There should be as much diversity as possible among those churches on whose communal identities the curriculum focuses. Ideally, any community that chooses to call itself a Christian church might be a candidate for that role. But even if all the communities selected belonged to the same denomination, the effects of social and economic stratification on our society allow a variety of communal identities. This diversity is important because it enables the curriculum to resist becoming ideologically captive. A curriculum becomes ideologically captive when it leads to an understanding of Christian identity, both communal and individual, that uncritically assimilates the interests and commitments of particular segments of society. But a curriculum could resist this if it included a study and comparison of different Christian communities.

Although two kinds of stories are told about a particular local church, they play different roles in living as part of a local church. The biblical narratives and the nonnarrative sections of scripture that comment on the narratives perform functions the other kind of narrative does not, namely, calling the community into being, nurturing a common life, and providing the basis for the continual criticism and reform of that common life. A church's communal identity is shown in human actions lived between memory and hope. It is a response, not so much to an experience of present grace, as to an experience of trust in and loyalty to a memory of past grace and a hope for and love of a promised future grace. A church's communal identity is called into being and sustained as it is reminded of this promise by the use of

---

[2] See my essay "On the Christian Congregation," earlier in this volume, for a more extensive discussion of the characteristics of a Christian congregation.

biblical narratives in its common life and in worshiping, preaching, educating, pastoral caring, and arguing.

A church is also constantly faithless to it own communal identity. The ways in which it speaks and acts are inadequate or inappropriate responses to the gift that calls it into being and gives it its identity. Dorothy Day, who had reason to know, wrote into her journal one day a line she had read in Romano Guardini: "The church is the cross on which Jesus is crucified." Precisely because they call the community into being and nurture its common life, the biblical narratives also function as the norm by which this faithlessness is brought to light. And the community may use these narratives as the basis for decisions regarding its reform. Of the two kinds of stories through which a church describes its communal identity, it is the biblical stories that function normatively.

A theological curriculum could be a course of studies if it addressed the communal identity of Christian communities as conveyed in these two kinds of stories. This would help determine how particular courses should be conceived and taught and the kinds of methodologies that they should use.

Except for basic language courses, courses in all subjects could address two questions: Who are we? and How is our communal identity best nurtured and best kept under critical scrutiny?

In exploring the first question, a course would use its subject matter and appropriate methodologies to explain one or the other of the two kinds of narrative through which congregations describe their communal identities. The question would provide the boundaries within which courses in Bible, church history, historical theology, systematic theology, and the sociology and psychology of religion would be designed and taught. This would not erode the scholarly integrity of such courses, as they would deal with the same subject matters as always, using the same scholarly methods. But this all would be used to explain the different ways in which Christian communities have used biblical narratives to describe their identities and what they say about themselves when they do so.

Such courses would emphasize the promissory force of those narratives and what happens to Christian communities when it is forgotten. As Christopher Morse argued in his study of Jürgen Moltmann, many of the narratives that are normative for Christian communal identity have the logical force of open-ended promises.[3] When that has been forgotten, the community acts as a *closed* system, as though it were identified by negation of the host culture. Such a community sees itself as drawing people out of the world and into the community, protecting its Christian identity from erosion by identity-shaping forces of communities outside the church, and preserv-

[3] Christopher Morse, *The Logic of Promise in Moltmann's Theology* (Philadelphia: Fortress Press, 1979).

ing the deposit of past grace from loss or misinterpretation. But when the promissory force of the normative narratives is kept in the forefront, the complex of human actions that comprises a church's common life is an *open* system. It is open to the life of its host culture, concerned for the well-being of that culture and anticipating the fulfillment of God's promised presence in that culture.

It is because a church's common life is an open system that a theological curriculum addressing the question Who are we? must also study the non-biblical stories that Christian communities tell about themselves. Indeed, it is because the narratives' promissory force requires the community to be open to the world that the biblical narratives themselves require that the nonbiblical stories also be studied. For these are the stories by which the community describes itself as part of its host culture, fulfilling social and psychological functions that are sometimes peripheral and sometimes central to that culture.

Here the methods of the human sciences become relevant. A church's identity as described in nonbiblical stories provides the subject matter for research and courses in the sociology and social psychology of religion as applied to Christian communities. And here is where descriptions of Christian communities using the third person plural rather than the first person plural find a place in the theological curriculum. Perhaps even more beneficial, as is suggested by James Hopewell's research, would be to use ethnographic methods to study the common life of Christian congregations accepted as cultures in their own right. Some of these methodologies are also being used to study the other kind of identifying stories, that is the biblical narratives, in the work of Wayne Meeks in New Testament and Robert Wilson in Old Testament. Indeed, the attempt to focus the theological curriculum on the communal identity of churches seems to call for some such change in methodology as well, some revision of the curriculum in which the historians have long had hegemony. By considering the stories that communities tell about themselves, a nonhistorical methodology would enable the focus of teaching and learning to fall on the community's sense of its identity rather than on descriptions of its identity that use a priori theoretical constructs. Only by combining communal self-description with its self-description through biblical narratives can a theological curriculum concentrate on the identities of actual concrete churches, thereby making it a genuine course of studies and not just an assemblage of discrete courses.

If the theological curriculum examined the communal identities of Christian communities and thereby became a genuine course of study, individual courses would need to be designed and taught in accordance with the second question: How is our communal identity best nurtured and best kept under critical scrutiny? That is, questions in pastoral theology, broadly conceived, would provide the boundaries within which courses in all subjects would be designed and taught. By questions in pastoral theology, I mean questions about how Christian identity is nurtured and illuminated; how the personal capacities, dispositions, attitudes, and passions that mark such a life are learned; and how one comes to regard oneself, one's neighbors, and the social and natural contexts of one's life in appropriate ways. In particular, such questions need to be asked about the roles played in nurturing and illuminating Christian identity by the two kinds of stories through which Christian communities describe their identities.

The stories play these roles when they are used in the various actions that comprise the community's common life. Now among the complex of human actions that comprise the common life of a Christian community, two distinctions must be made. First, some actions can be described only by reference to those goals they seek to accomplish, whereas others can be described only as actions carried out for their own sake. Second, some of these actions are intrinsic to the community's identity, whereas others are ingredient to that identity only insofar as they are rooted in or address other actions that are intrinsic to it. The identity of a community and its members is nurtured not merely by their engaging in these actions but also by the way that their engaging in these actions is explicitly or implicitly informed by these stories.

The actions of a church's common life that are intrinsic to its communal identity are those carried out for their own sake rather than for the sake of realizing a goal, namely, the actions of glorifying God. Doxological acts, the actions in worshiping God, are those through which the community creates its identity. They are performed for their own sake. Doxology is not a goal-oriented undertaking; it is not instrumental to any further end. Doxological acts also are the actions by which the community nurtures its identity. For it is in the act of praising God that persons assume the identity described in the biblical stories, commit themselves to those identities, and acknowledge their intentions to live that identity. Thus begins their acquisition of the personal capacities, dispositions, attitudes, passions, and beliefs that will shape their lives. But they do not worship just to shape this identity; rather, they evoke and nurture this Christian identity, both communal and individual, by doing other things, and not as goals in themselves.

Clearly, other actions are also important to the community's common life because they support the intrinsic actions. These are goal-oriented actions. They range from religious education, and especially catechesis, to the appointment of committees and fund raising. The community's identity will be further nurtured and defined when these actions are informed by the narratives that describe this identity.

Some goal-oriented actions are essential to the common life of a church not because they help support but because they are rooted in acts of praising God. Among them, two are particularly important. In acts of glorifying God, the community commits itself to acting and speaking in ways that are appropriate responses to God, or more specifically, appropriate responses to the modes in which God was present and promises to be present. This entails, first, an act of critical self-reflection or self-assessment: Are our current forms of speech and action faithful to our communal identity? In such an act, the biblical narratives that shape the community's corporate identity play a normative role. They describe the community's real identity, the identity that the community has even when it is faithless to itself.

In order to determine whether its current forms of speech and action are faithful to its identity, the community needs some formulations of its identity to use as criteria against which to judge and, if necessary, reform itself. Much of the church's theological task is to propose such formulations. Accordingly, courses designed and taught within the boundaries of the pastoral theological question (How is the communal identity of a church best nurtured and best kept under critical scrutiny?) become discussions of constructive theological proposals. Here a theological education designed to study a church's communal identity becomes a curriculum not only describing the church but also criticizing the church. Constructive theology is critical of churches and is reformist. It is rooted in pastoral theology, not vice versa. But this is true precisely because critical self-reflection is rooted in acts of praise. Theology, both pastoral and systematic, is rooted in doxology.

Acts of praising God entail a second kind of critical self-reflection. The nonbiblical narratives that a community tells about itself include narratives describing the social, political, economic, and cultural worlds that are the community's context. When the community in worship acts and speaks in ways that are appropriate responses to God, it also commits itself to a critical assessment of the world of which it is a part. The community must ask whether such patterns of behavior—dominant value commitments, societally encouraged attitudes, and the like—are constant with the modes in which God has been and promises to be present in those worlds. Here self-reflection critical of a church's common life and reflection critical of the culture of which it is a part will often come together. When the description of a community's identity given in the biblical narratives is compared with the ways in which the community is actually speaking and acting and with the behaviors, values, and attitudes celebrated by the community's host culture, then—to be concrete—questions about racist, sexist, and nationalistic attitudes, behavior, and power arrangements, both inside and outside the community must be considered in courses focused on those narratives. In short, a curriculum that is a course of studies because it considers the communal identity of Christian churches will contain courses designed and taught with such questions of social ethics in mind.

But this is not because goal-oriented social action is intrinsic to the community's identity. Acts of praise that are not goal oriented are what is intrinsic. Social criticism and socially responsible action are rooted in that. Social imperatives in the Christian life are not based on assertions of indicatives but on acts of doxology. For three reasons I believe that it is important to stress this. It protects against a false and ideological bifurcation between "spiritual" worship and "worldly" social action. It preserves the vitality of socially responsible action inherent in worship. And it makes clear in principle that there is freedom in the Christian community for disagreement about what counts as socially responsible action. When the identity of the church is defined in terms of goal-oriented, socially responsible action, then it is difficult to distinguish between being faithless to the community's identity and dissenting from the majority opinion within the community about what counts as socially responsible action. The traditional, and apparently conservative, insistence that the church's identity lies in acts of worship that may appear irrelevant to the world's injustice, bondage, and suffering turns out in principle to be the most radical way of construing the church's identity if and when it emphasizes critical self-reflection, because of the energy and freedom it generates for social criticism and social action.

Learned Pastors

I have sketched how a curriculum might be a course of study rather than an aggregate of courses, by focusing on the identity of Christian communities. I have suggested how that focus would affect the ends for which individual courses were designed and taught. I have pointed out such a curriculum's implications for the methodologies that would prevail in theological education. And I have proposed all this as an alternative to the individualism of most of the current proposals for reforming the theological curriculum, which emphasize preparing the individual student to fill specialized roles in churches.

My contention is that a theological curriculum focusing on the identity of particular churches would produce "learned pastors." Not all of them would assume specialized roles in the common life of a church. Indeed, one of the major strengths of this proposal, in my view, is that it would prevent the clergy-laity distinction from becoming the curriculum's organizing structural feature.

I use the phrase *learned pastor* to refer to any person, whether or not ordained, who has become particularly knowledgeable about the human actions that constitute the common life of particular Christian communities. Those actions are the work of all the people of God, not simply of the clergy. The theological curriculum thus should be a course of study that enhances the capacities of those who move through it to engage in these actions.

Here the world *learned* has a special sense that is appropriate to what constitutes the life of a church. Learned in reference to the clergy (as in the phrase *learned professions*) once got its force from the fact that most people had little more than a rudimentary education. By the end of the nineteenth century, learned had come to characterize someone who had acquired specialized research skills and was educated in the lore, bibliography, and current state of an academic specialty. In theological circles the methodology was generally historical, regardless of the research field. The first sense of

learned, therefore, is an anachronism in a society with generally higher
levels of education. The second sense of learned has increasingly been in
tension with capacities needed in the life of Christian communities. It is a
tension felt and expressed in persistent complaints that historically oriented
biblical and theological studies are irrelevant to the practice of ministry.
There is something to that complaint. What I have been proposing about an
alternative way to order the curriculum is an attempt to suggest that nonetheless there need not be anything to it. I have proposed a course of study
through which persons could become learned in a tradition. Through that
curriculum they could increase the capacities needed by those engaging in
the actions that comprise the common life of a Christian church. The stories
that give form and direction to these actions are handed down or "tradi-
tioned" within a community from generation to generation. So to be learned
in that tradition is not only to be master of a body of information but to be
capable of participating in a tradition of enactments *in a reflective and self-
critical way*. These capacities are in some degree common property to
everyone in the community—capacities for faith, hope, love, justice, mercy,
and critical reflection. Hence they require knowledge of the theological
norms that may be used in criticism and of the biblical materials on which
they are based. Here historical-critical biblical study is both relevant and
important, but now in the context of the tradition that constitutes a church's
common life rather than in the context of the tradition of historical research.

To label as pastors persons who are learned in this way is to stress that
the capacities they have acquired through their course of study are capacities
to empower others in the same way. It is correct to call these persons
"leaders" in the church. But it is important to emphasize that Christian
identity brings with it specific modalities of leadership. An identity that is
shaped as an appropriate response to the mode in which God has been and
promises to be present according to biblical narratives requires a mode of
leadership that does not keep people dependent but, rather, enables them to
be more fully themselves in their own response to God's presence. This does
not deny the differences among members of a community. But the acknowl-
edgement of differences does not necessitate superordinate-subordinate relationships.

To be concerned for others in a way that empowers and encourages their
Christian identity is to have a pastoral relationship with them. To do this in a
reflective and self-critical way means raising pastoral theology questions. If
they are normative questions, pastoral theology issues will generate theological questions. And the formulation of theological norms is guided by the
stories through which the community gives a normative account of its identity. It is because of that movement from pastoral quandaries to constructive
theology to narrative renderings of communal identity that the theological
curriculum can most effectively be made a course of studies if it focuses on
the communal identity of Christian churches.

FRIENDS IN THE FAMILY:
CHURCH, SEMINARY, AND THEOLOGICAL EDUCATION

Marjorie Hewitt Suchocki

Why is there so often tension between churches and seminaries? Although most people may not believe the cliché that one must be wary of seminaries lest they "destroy the faith" of the neophyte seminarian, the criticism is like a persistent undertow that works beneath the surface, eroding the supporting structures between seminary and church. Nor have seminaries been free of a mistrust of the churches, particularly in their evaluation of the churches' quality of faith and theological reflection. Although the church and seminary must be interdependent, the constructive aspect of this relationship depends on their basic esteem for each other. By using a model that fosters this esteem, the church and seminary may serve each other more constructively and find more effective ways to cooperate in preparing persons for leadership in the church.

My thesis is that an implicit sexism has hindered this relationship between church and seminary, and that attention to this problem can correct the aforementioned difficulties. Ideologically the church has been identified as feminine, and so it suffers from some of the same negative stereotypes as do women. This has had two results. The first is theological, manifested in ecclesiologies that exalt the ideal church and denigrate the actual church, much like the ideological dualism between Mary and ordinary women. The second result is sociological, as seen in the hierarchical dualism between seminary and church, paralleling the sexisit dichotomies between intellect and body. Both of these results have contributed to the mutual mistrust just cited, and to distortions in theology and theological education.

Feminists have been quite clear in objections to thinking that equates God with masculinity and humanity with femininity, with the implication that as God is with humanity, so is man with woman. The dichotomy of characteristics in this dualism is that qualities such as power, wisdom, and holiness belong on the divine side, and qualities of weakness, sinfulness, and ignorance are attributed to humanity. The divine is steadfast and changeless, whereas the human is faithless and changing. In the translation into social categories, men have absorbed or have been afflicted with the norm of attaining divine qualities, and women have been assigned the task of symbolizing human qualities. Men, like God, are to rule and have dominion over the earth; women, like humanity, are to be submissive to the godlike representatives of the divine, men. Although one can draw the parallels in extreme ways, one can also find exceptions to this analogy. Yet it has affected the images of men and women in literature and in culture, and both women and men have responded to the feminist critique by rewriting theology so that it is more egalitarian.

What has not received particular attention is that the church and women both have had to endure such sexist negativity. Instead, feminists tend to see the church as the oppressor, with women the victims. *The Church and the Second Sex*, by Mary Daly, is one of many examples of this kind of thinking. But the situation may be more complicated. Insofar as the church is under-stood to be exercising its intellectual capacities through the agency of clergy or scholars, masculinity and its so-called characteristics may indeed dominate, but the church as a whole is typified as "the Bride of Christ," "the body of Christ," and feminine. One is reminded of the old characterization of the soul as feminine vis-a-vis its submission to God, but masculine vis-a-vis its rulership of the body. Just as the intellect/soul is deemed masculine in its responsibility for the body, the body is deemed feminine in its submissiveness to the intellect/soul. Applied to the church, as a ruling hierarchy it is male, but as a ruled body it is female and therefore by "nature" is submissive to its hierarchy.

Thus the familiar dualism of sexism may work against not only women but in another variant against the institutional structure of the church itself. One could assume that in preseminary times, this institutional dualism divided the dominant masculine, intellectualized clergy and the feminized laity. In our own time, with the rise of seminaries, the same division may now exist between the masculinized academy and the feminized church. In this dualism, the local churches suffer condescension and subtle forms of denigration, and the academies suffer as ghettos of scholarship increasingly distanced from the very people they intend to serve. Both situations are harmful to theological education.

The negative feminine stereotype can be seen in the church in the way that theologians address two of the traditional marks of the church, unity and holiness. (The other two marks—catholicity and apostolicity—are treated more often in relation to the church's masculine hierarchy than the congregations themselves and hence are not so often included in the negative feminine stereotypes.) In unity and holiness, the good is projected onto transcendent realms, and the negative remains the inherent property of the real church.

Unity, for example, is often seen as a consensus on fundamental doctrine so that each church might commune with every other. In the Lima text of the Faith and Order Commission of the World Council of Churches, unity is expressed as a "goal of visible unity in one faith and one eucharistic fellowship expressed in worship and common Life in Christ, in order that the world might believe."[1] This goal is held as a judgment against the church, so that the actual situation of churches that hold to quite diverse expressions of faith, mutually exclusive celebrations of the eucharist, and divisions over the meaning and mode of baptism is seen as part of the sin of the church. In the words of Wolfhart Pannenberg, "In Jesus Christ the unity of all Christians (is) already a reality," and the fact of diversity among the churches is "an expression of lack of faith and . . . resistance to the working of the Holy Spirit."[2] The good is projected to transcendent realms, and the dregs describe the church's reality. Further, the Lima texts state a cherished assumption that were the church only to manifest a unity of faith and sacraments, then the world would be persuaded to become Christian. This assumption is peculiar, given the general antipathy toward totalitarian systems, which presumably impose one correct manner of thought and action on their subjects. One wonders whether those who proclaim that "the world might believe" if "unity in one faith and one eucharistic fellowship" were manifest have ever checked to find out whether indeed there is any scorn or even concern over the fact that Christian churches exist in a variety of communions and denominations. The "scandal" of church diversity is more likely to be a scandal not to the world, or to ordinary church members, but to officials within the churches' power structures who look not to the reality of historical churches to understand what Christian unity might be, but to an abstract notion of oneness.

Holiness fares no better, for traditionally holiness in the sense of purity is located in Jesus Christ, whereas sinfulness describes the churches. In *The Church*, Hans Küng describes the tension and its resolution in a manner typical of the tradition. He first lists the ways in which the church's holiness cannot be understood. It is not a Donatism, with some members of the church counted as pure and holy, and others as sinners; holiness does not belong to an idealized church with the visible church counted as sinful; and finally, holiness is not a division of the church's members that makes each member holy in some respects and sinful in others. Küng also states that he wishes to talk about the real church and not some ideal church; indeed, he seems to agree with the feminist agenda I am proposing.

But when Küng moves from what he believes holiness not to be to what he considers it to be, one wonders whether he is very far removed from the false images of holiness that he decries. Like the Donatists, Küng finds a sense of holiness in a "set apartness of the holy," only instead of making the separation within the church, he draws it between the church and the world.

---

[1] The World Council of Churches, *Baptism, Eucharist and Ministry*, Faith and Order Paper No. 111 (Geneva: World Council of Churches, 1982), 1.

[2] Wolfhart Pannenberg, *The Church*, trans. Keith Crim (Philadelphia: Westminster Press, 1983), 23, 25.

Although he does not see the holiness of this removed church as separating the ideal and the real, he nevertheless does view this holiness as from above. This "above," however, is God rather than the ideal church: "We must conclude that the holiness of the Church does not stem from its members and their moral and religious behavior . . . We do not simply believe in the holy Church, but believe in God who makes the church holy . . . This holiness, being the work of God's spirit among [us], is not accessible to us or controllable by us; it is not something seen, but something that is revealed to those who in faith open their hearts . . ." There is, then, something within the believer that is native to the self, namely, sin; and struggling with this is a new, sanctifying, and holy Spirit seeking to transform the sinner. The work, however, is problematic enough that "to the believer alone is revealed the fact that this people which looks so familiar to other peoples and communities in the world, and yet is fundamentally so dissimilar, is illumined by the holiness of God; [the believer] alone can know that within this externally so imperfect building the Spirit of God [in] holiness dwells, that this frail and often wounded body reflects the holiness of the Kyrios."[3] Although Küng began by bemoaning a holiness that relates only to the ideal, the subtleties of his own avoidance of such a position surely question his success. "Always holy and always sinful" finally means the God who is always holy and the church that is always sinful. Like the dialectic so familiar to feminists, good comes to the feminine from outside itself and in no sense is to be equated with anything in its essential nature.

Is there not a disquieting similarity between the holiness of the church and the way in which women achieved value in the patristic centuries of the church? To Küng, with echoes of Luther, the righteousness of the church is an "alien righteousness" that moves the sinful church toward conformity with itself until finally it becomes a "little Christ," purified in its ultimate transformation. Likewise, if women in the early church opened themselves to ascetic transformation, they could overcome the impediment of their femaleness; that is, they could become male. Then as now, only by conforming to something not herself could a woman attain value. Likewise, the diversity and ambiguity that belong to churches existing in time and space are discounted; only by conforming with the nontemporal, transcendent Christ can they achieve value. How can women and the church ever be valued for themselves? They must always be what they, in principle, cannot be in order to win the approval of men or a masculine God.

Thus in traditional doctrines of the church the positive aspects of unity and holiness are projected to the transcendent God or Christ, and disunity and sinfulness remain the visible signs of the feminine "Bride." The church is valued for what it essentially is not. Though feminists have noted this dynamic with regard to women, they have left it largely untouched with

[3] Hans Küng, *The Church* (Garden City, New York: Doubleday, 1967), 417, 419.

regard to the church. But if the dynamic works against women's interests, it may have equally negative results for the churches.

Some of these negative results are manifested in attitudes. Academies often show a subtle sense of superiority toward the churches to which they are in some sense accountable. Medical and law school faculties seem to have a high regard for those practitioners whom they once taught, but can we say the same thing of the regard in which theological faculties hold the clergy who were once their students? One could speculate that once the graduates leave the seminary and enter the world of the churches, they cease to be clearly identified with the academy and are in fact immersed—incarnate?—in that negative feminine reality, the church. The clergy, meanwhile, having come from the male (or formerly male!) world of the academy, are themselves in an ambivalent position. They are asociated with the superior masculine world of the academy in the eyes of their parishioners and therefore rule over the feminine laity, but they are associated with the feminine church in the eyes of the academy and therefore have lost the status belonging to the purely masculine sphere.

Consider also another comparison between medical schools and theological schools. Both require their students to undergo a form of internship: the residency in medicine and field education and/or internship in theological education. The residency appears to be highly valued by the medical profession and is in no sense regarded as inferior to the class work required of the fledgling physician. Rather, the class work seems to culminate in the residency. The field education, however, occupies no similarly elevated place in seminary curricula. Indeed, it is often viewed as marginal to the "truly academic" work of the classroom and as an appendage to the student's education, rather than as the culmination or heart of the process. The internship is likewise regarded with less than unmitigated enthusiasm, with some faculty complaining that such internships diminish the student's zest for the more "demanding" studies of the academy. These attitudes are odd, as we are seeking to provide leadership in the church. Why, then, are the first attempts to exercise that leadership disparaged?

The ambiguity of my comments arises from the fact that the seminaries are institutions of the church, existing to serve the church. Any devaluation of the church would thus seem to be a devaluation of the seminary as well, but the long-standing sexist dualism of intellect and soul versus body offers a rationale for this situation. Insofar as the academy identifies itself as intellect in the sexist sense, it "naturally" rules over the feminine body. In such a situation one can denigrate the body, even while identifying with that body.

In a peculiar twist of language, however, the seminary can also assert that it exists to serve the church. However, when such service is applied to those in hierarchical control, it takes on meaning quite different from that of the service to be rendered by the feminized church. Although servant leadership was a powerful symbol for egalitarian relationships of mutual enrichment in the early church, it was quickly transformed in the emergence of a hierarchical structure. Leadership was no longer qualified by servanthood but instead absorbed servanthood, until being a servant in the church became synonymous with being a lord in the church, with power over others. Thus in the distorted symbolism of patriarchy, the seminary as servant to the church can easily imply a superiority over the church.

Liberation theology has taught us that solidarity with the oppressed is necessary if we are to correct oppressive symbolism. The close association already existing between academy and church indicates that we must not only affirm our solidarity, but seek a mutuality that will turn our closeness into an enriching relationship. How can this mutuality be created, given the pervasive influence of the hierarchical and sexist imagery? I suggest that we begin to replace or reinterpret the body imagery that implicitly fosters sexism in dominant-submissive relations, and that we use nondualistic relationships between seminary and church as models. The body imagery, after all, is metaphorical rather than literal. Might there be another metaphor free from the sexist connotations of the body imagery and more suitable to the complex relations between seminary and church? The church is a society far more complex than that of an individual; in its ecumenical diversity it spans various traditions and values. Perhaps the image of a family rather than of a single individual is more appropriate to the church, speaking to its relational and interpersonal nature. A family knows a diversity of its members and yet a unity of general background and interpersonal commitment; likewise the church exists in a plurality even while naming a unity of heritage and commitment. If we apply the metaphor of family to seminary and church, we can further interpret the relationship as that between an adult daughter or son and a parent. Whereas once there as a hierarchical relationship, there now is a rich combination of mutuality, friendship, and partnership. In the adult relationship there is no competition over which partner has the greater value; rather, each values both the other and oneself. In such a matrix of value, creativity and work can flourish.

If such a metaphor were applied to the seminary and the church, each would acknowledge the familial relationship that binds them. The hierarchical imagery of sexism that assigns primacy to the intellectual academy would be overturned, for the church precedes the academy, and not the academy the church. Historically, the church generated scholarship and established educational models to ensure, among other things, educated leadership within the church. A dominant contemporary form of that educational model is the seminary, which in turn has devised its own standards and rules of discourse to ensure educational quality. The seminary has "come of age" and relates most effectively to the church not in hierarchy but in mutuality, as friends within the family.

If such a metaphor were the model, the church would no longer be judged simply by the theologies of the academy, but the church and the seminary together would generate theology. In the current mode of theologizing, the seminary succumbs far too easily to the temptation to develop idealized notions of the church against which the real churches of our cities, towns, and countrysides are too often found wanting. The concrete churches are frequently strangers to the abstract ecclesiologies of the academy, and the distance of value or identification feeds into sexist problems. If the church and seminary developed ecclesiologies in conversation with each other, our doctrines might emerge from critical reflection together upon our experiences. Such doctrines might refer more recognizably to our realities.

For example, the vibrancy of the many different forms of Christianity might be regarded as a challenge to the theological assumption that unity requires a common interpretation of the sacraments for the sake of intercommunion. Other models of unity that build upon theological (and therefore sacramental) diversity would commend themselves, and modes of unity that in fact already connect the churches might be discovered. With regard to holiness, we might consider that if the actual church were as sinful as interpretations of holiness indicate, it is a wonder that the church has existed as long as it has. Perhaps it is the case that the demand upon the church to be holy is a demand that the church actualizes in its struggles for justice and well-being in the world. A holiness interpreted as justice might well be a temporal quality the church can and must exercise. If we remain convinced that we are members of "one, holy, catholic, and apostolic church," can we not form our understanding of those attributes from reflective discussions together? The theologies thus developed would emerge from the reality of the church and in turn be tested by that reality. Theology would be a dynamic process illumining our living identity as the church.

This is not to imply that theology only mirrors the contemporary church. Texts, traditions, and philosophical thought remain the stuff with which we work, but texts, traditions, and philosophical thought are not self-tested in a circle, such as Barth's "cloud cuckooland" or Whitehead's never-landing "aeroplane." The theologies we create with those tools must touch our experience in the contemporary world, and a cornerstone of that experience is the concreteness of the church. To take the churches seriously enough to work together to generate and revise our theologies is to gain from this family partnership of friends.

If theology gains in a relationship of friendship between theologian and church, the academy and the church will also gain. If "family friendship" is a model for academy-church relations, then the church will be a conversation partner in theological education, not only the subject of theological education. Nor will the academy be seen as simply echoing the church's contemporary emphases on belief and action, yea-saying like an obedient puppet each dictum of the church. Friends are not clones but partners, each with a distinctive task. The academy is that partner with a twofold calling, one of which is to understand the heritage of our Christianity with all the scholarly honesty at its command. From this understanding, in conversation with the churches, new formulations of the faith may be proposed; new calls to the Reign of God may be indicated. The second calling, closely related to the first, is to share these studies with those preparing to be leaders in the church so that these persons shall be well equipped for that leadership, and able in their own turn to share the empowering texts and traditions with the congregations. Thus the academy is the partner that contributes its scholarship to the church's own dynamic identity, constructively criticizing that identity. The church's calling is to live in the vibrancy and ministry of the faith community, informed by what it has been and what it can be in faithful response to the call of God toward the world's well-being. The church's task is to fit the general call for well-being to the particularities of its own community and locale, and to participate denominationally and ecumenically in meeting global needs for well-being. The church's particularization of ministry requires that the church should know the world's professions and crafts and ways—a knowledge brought to the community through the laity involved in these works and ways. Through such knowledge, each congregation is uniquely equipped to define and address contemporary needs. Thus the church is the place through which the Reign of God finds an opportunity for incarnation in each new moment, and therefore the church is a locus for the testing and development of theology relating to the Reign of God. The church is the partner that contributes the particularities and concreteness of ministry, from which it constructively criticizes theology.

Each partner helps the other perform its task more faithfully. Each offers not only supplementary knowledge but critical help as well. The academy, with its tendency to abstractions and arrogance, can be kept humble and honest by the concrete particularity of Christianity in its presentness. The church, with its tendency to become immersed in the needs and concerns of the present, is called to the criticism of its wider heritage and future by the faithfulness of the academy.

Such a description of a family-friendship model of relationships between the seminary and the church risks being just one more form of idealistic rhetoric. What concrete changes would occur if the seminary and church took seriously a nondualistic model, valuing the contributions and cooperation of each other? Several immediate implications come to mind. First, field education might move to a more central role in the curriculum, but perhaps in a revised form using the concept of teaching congregations. Second, the Ph.D model of teaching that characterizes many Master of Divinity classrooms might be supplemented with the Doctor of Ministry model of teaching that has emerged as faculty and pastors relate academic disciplines to ministry.

Given this stronger valuation of churches, seminaries should reconsider the role of congregations in preparing persons for ministry. The opportunity for this in the current curricular model is the field education program, where seminarians are placed in churches in the student's second year of study. In these programs, pastors supervise the seminarians' work. Although ideally the seminarian has an opportunity to work in all modes of the church's life, in practice youth work is often the seminarian's principal responsibility. Ideally, the congregation should help guide the seminarian's work, but usually this guidance falls to the pastor and seminary supervisor. Ideally, this experience in the church should be brought back to each classroom in the seminary, raising questions concerning the applicability and/or transmission of course materials to the ministry. But if raised at all, such questions are usually limited to courses in education, administration, preaching, and pastoral care. With a renewed valuation of the congregation as the living community of faith, the field education program could be restructured to see that its ideal becomes its practice.

This could happen in several ways. The field education could parallel the entire seminary experience, with every course designed to call attention to the material's relevance to actual communities of faith. Currently, this can best be done by maximizing the opportunities presented by student appointments as sole pastor, but there is no reason why assistant positions could not also be lengthened and related to the whole seminary curriculum. The role of the congregation during this period for either the student pastor or the student assistant could be one of partnership with the seminary in preparing the person for leadership in the church. The congregation would be teacher to the student, working primarily (but not exclusively) through a small lay committee appointed for such service. The work of this committee and congregation would not simply be to give critical feedback to the seminarian, but also to help the student apply class materials to ministry. Syllabi from classes would be shared with the committee, and papers written for classes might receive a first critique from the committee. If the paper were rewritten in light of this critique, both editions would be turned in to the seminary professor in order that the professor might judge the effectiveness of the materials in the community of faith, as well as the student's growth in ministry.

The role of a teaching congregation goes beyond interaction with the seminarian's course work. The congregation also reviews and clarifies its own understanding of its mission. This includes reviewing its own history and its denominational mission goals; studying its wider community's demographics, opportunities, and needs; analyzing its own congregational resources, and formulating a statement of its missional intent in light of this study. Leadership in this process comes primarily from the lay committee (or pastor if the seminarian is serving as an assistant), but the whole congregation must be involved. This is particularly important, as the varying skills and abilities of the congregation are assessed in light of perceived needs in the congregation and its community. The seminarian is both resource person and student throughout this process: resource person, in that materials from the seminary classes can guide the congregation's work, and student, in that the seminarian's participation in this process contributes to his or her understanding of the church's identity and mission as a living community of faith.

The seminarian, of course, would feel the impact of the seminary-church partnership most dramatically. Instead of living in two worlds, the world of the academy and the world of the church, the seminarian would bridge these worlds. Scholarship and the communal life of faith would demand integration in new ways and carry over into a lifelong ministry. To facilitate this integration, the seminary should institute small faculty-led student discussion groups that meet weekly to discuss the church and seminary experience, raising questions about the relation of course work to the life of the church.

If my rough sketch of a field education program were refined and adapted by a seminary, it would have to include the following. First, the seminary and church should approach such a partnership with a commitment to pray for each other. Such a commitment would hold before both partners the reality that it is God to whom both are accountable, and that by the grace of God there is empowerment for the work. Second, the seminary should consider holding workshops for congregational committees in which the overall curriculum could be reviewed and the relation among the congregation, student, and course work could be discussed. Third, the seminary and church should devise methods of mutual evaluation, in which accomplishments could be measured by expectations.

A program using teaching congregations could benefit the student, church, and seminary. The student would be required to relate materials on texts and traditions to the life of the church and to lead the church in its own critical appropriation of its heritage as it continued to create tradition in its own life. The church could become a touchstone for the seminary's scholarship and a mentor as the seminary continues to struggle with how best to prepare persons for leadership in the church. How do we offer honest scholarship to the church, conveying the texts and the traditions both critically and faithfully to the communities who own and are owned by them? And the seminary could likewise become a mentor to the church, calling on the church to use its heritage and to renew its mission in the community and world.

Partnership between the seminary and church would also benefit teaching methods. Ordinarily, professors model their classroom instruction on their own student experiences in Ph.D course work. However, such course work provides little opportunity for learning pedagogical methods, unless the degree is in that area of study. Instead, the focus is upon critical scholarship within a discipline. The goals of Ph.D study and M.Div. study are different enough to raise questions concerning the uncritical adoption of the classroom model of the one for the other. For example, Ph.D. study explores carefully one discipline, whereas M.Div. study must honor the multifaceted nature of ministry by introducing students to many different disciplines. In contrast to the Ph.D. student's advanced studies, the M.Div. student can go beyond the introductory level in only a few disciplines, given the variety of material to be covered within the three-year program. Ph.D. study measures its success by the student's ability to advance the scholarship of a discipline; M.Div. study measures its success by the student's ability to integrate course materials into personal and communal lives of faith, applying that faith to personal, communal, and global issues. Ph.D. study culminates in the written word, whereas M.Div. study culminates in the proclaimed and lived word. Ph.D. study prepares a person to take his or her place in a community of scholars, whereas M.Div. study prepares a person to take his or her place in a community of faith. Although there is some overlap in the materials of both forms of study—the same books may be read in both programs—the intentions of the degrees are different enough to raise this question: Should the teaching methods be the same in both degree programs? Would a change in teaching methods enhance the effectiveness of M.Div. studies?

An answer to this issue grows out of the educational program that has grown so rapidly in the past two decades, the Doctor of Ministry degree. Here the interaction is not with the congregation directly (although all programs involve the congregations to some degree), but between the clergy and professors. The teaching model emerging from this interaction is one in which course materials are examined in light of the practice of ministry, and the practice of ministry is examined in light of the course materials. The experience of ministry is central to the classroom dynamic. The gain to the professor is insight into the way that his or her discipline is or might be woven into the life of the church through pastoral leadership. This insight, carried over into the M.Div. classroom, can modify teaching styles so that M.Div. studies may more effectively achieve their goals.

This does not mean an end to lectures in M.Div. classes, but it does mean that every lecture will raise questions concerning the relation of the material to the ministry. Also, because students preparing for ministry presumably are engaged in the life of the church through work, field education, or their own membership, the congregation can provide the context for some of the class assignments. For example, professors could supplement a traditional paper or exam assignment with the requirement that the student work with that material in relation to the congregation. Questions emerging from congregational life might be raised in the classroom. Case studies might be used more frequently in class. Such teaching methods, learned from the D.Min. classroom, would model the seminary-church partnership in M.Div. classes, and convey to the students the high regard the seminary holds toward the churches.

If M.Div. teaching is thus affected by D.Min. experience, M.Div. students may also begin to look for the connections between congregational life and the studies designed to prepare them for the ordained ministry. Although the integration of materials and ministry may not reach the depth possible in a D. Min. class, to which the students bring years of experience in the ministry to their studies, it will nonetheless be established as a model. If students are expected to make these connections during their seminary study, relating congregational life to academic materials, is it not more likely that they will continue to relate academic materials to congregational life throughout their ministries? Teaching methods that bring such integration into the classroom may not guarantee such a result, but they will surely encourage it.

Underlying both of these suggestions is the supposition that seminaries and churches can overcome the hindrances, fostered by sexist devaluations of the feminine, that interfere with their effective cooperation. This calls for revaluing both our judgments concerning supposed male-female characteristics and our typing of nongendered realities by gender-specific names. As the seminary and church become more open to each other, they can dispell the myths and move toward a greater mutuality of purpose. The seminary and church are not antagonists competing for value but are partners and friends in a family. Each has its distinctive tasks, but each also has common concerns, one of which is the solid preparation of leadership within the church community. Only when this is done can pastors determine how Christian faith is shaped and shared in the concrete reality of a particular community, how they should work with the energies and abilities available in that community, how worshiping together can be more than a solo performance by preacher and singer before a passive audience and be the whole community's engagement in the energizing activity of worship. Neither the seminary nor the church alone can prepare persons for this kind of leadership. But together they can, finding in the process the joy of friendship in the family called church.

PART TWO
Disciplinary Perspectives on the Study of the Congregation

A STUDY OF THE CONGREGATION IN HISTORY

Jane Dempsey Douglass

My purpose in this chapter is to explore how the history of the church before about 1600 illuminates the actual culture of a twentieth-century local church and how, in turn, the life of that congregation might condition the manner in which I would teach in a Master of Divinity program.

Church History in Contemporary Local Churches

A topic like this cannot be discussed in relation to an abstraction like "local congregation." Therefore I shall make some observations drawn from years of experience with the forty-two congregations in my former presbytery in southern California. A few, some Hispanic and some Anglo, are nearing their centennial year. Many were founded thirty to forty years ago. Several, mostly congregations composed of new Asian immigrant groups, were organized in the last five years. All together, these congregations conduct worship in eight languages. They are "mainstream" Protestants whose pastors, both men and women, are seminary graduates.

The members of these congregations are as diverse as their churches. Many have changed denominations more than once in their lives, and others have a strong denominational identity that has lasted for many generations. Some are new Christians with no sense of churchly tradition. Several laypersons in these churches know more about some aspects of church history than do some of the pastors: a building contractor who reads in archaeology, a geologist who does research on British church history, a retired nursery-school teacher who reads Calvin, and women who read women's history.

Some of the pastors are genuinely interested in church history and use it effectively in their work. Occasionally, a pastor seems to have learned very little about church history and probably does more harm than good by perpetuating old falsehoods and prejudices under color of ecclesiastical authority. Generally, however, illumination from church history does not move easily from the pulpit to the pew. Church history rarely seems to be consciously incorporated into preaching as a teaching device, and it is much less common as the focus of education for either children or adults than are other elements of the theological curriculum. Many invitations that I have received to conduct adult-education programs in church history have been prefaced by the information that the minister wants such a program because that congregation has never had one. Pastors who regularly conduct Bible study groups and study groups on ethics, for example, will admit that they do not feel competent to teach church history. This observation supports the hypothesis that seminaries may not be teaching church history in ways that communicate to pastors the relevance and usefulness of a knowledge of church history to the real-life decisions of local congregations.

Yet the perceptions of church history held by pastors and lay people constantly shape the life of local congregations. In some cases, these perceptions are factually wrong or inappropriate, but that does not necessarily diminish the fierceness with which they are advanced as truth. In committee meetings and planning sessions, church members act according to their beliefs about church history, particularly in a tradition like mine that takes history very seriously.

Let me illustrate this point with an example. In 1970, my denomination published a new hymnal that included suggested liturgies. The service proposed for regular Sunday use is in fact a eucharistic service that must be abbreviated if communion is not to be celebrated. This service includes many traditional eucharistic formulas that were not commonly used in the local congregations under discussion. Indeed, the minister of one of these churches asked me to meet with the worship commission soon after the hymnal's publication because the commission strongly opposed his suggestion to try the proposed liturgy. When I met with the commission and asked about the reasons for their opposition, I was told angrily that the minister was trying to persuade them to use a "catholic" service that was absolutely contrary to the Reformed tradition of worship. Their sense of tradition was offended by both the idea of weekly communion and the unfamiliar style of the service. Further questions revealed that the commission had not read the denomination's official directory for worship and that nearly half of the commission members had joined the denomination only in the past five years. I must assume that the minister realized that historical issues were at stake, since he called in a historian. But he himself had made no effort at all to teach the commission about the history of worship in the church before the Reformation or in the Reformed tradition. Given the intensity of the discussion, I was happy to find that an hour and a half of education in the history of worship could change the atmosphere. The commission members became curious about the history of Reformed worship and the broader tradition, and they were open to a fresh consideration of the question. They had been sincere in defending their vision of the tradition but recognized that they had limited experience in that tradition. Once they realized that historical study would help them make pressing decisions, they were willing to begin.

This episode and many others have led me to believe that congregations really do care about their role in handing down tradition. They tend to be handicapped, however, by a short and narrow view of tradition. Understanding at least the outlines of the history of worship would aid decision making at the local level. Here, in my tradition, a worship commission made up of lay people along with the local session, composed of elders and ministers, must work together in planning their worship. These people have often grown up in different ecclesiastical traditions, experiencing a variety of practices that seem "right" to them, even though they cannot explain the function of the practices or the theology underlying them. But in this ecumenical age, more options are available to the planners of worship. The shape of sanctuaries, the style of vestments, the biblical translation to be read aloud, and the language of the prayers will not be automatically determined by tradition but must be consciously chosen. Some of the questions arising from these choices have become emotionally charged: whether to use an inclusive-language lectionary, for example. If one takes a short view of history, the change to inclusive language might look like a rash innovation. But if one knows something of the history of repeated change to ensure worship in the vernacular, such a change might seem like a more traditional choice. Some understanding of the reasons for change in the long history of worship has helped many congregations make decisions that have some theological consistency.

Another set of questions being asked in local congregations focuses on issues of social action. Should the church, a "spiritual" organization, become involved in "political" matters? On the surface this looks like an ethical question. But again and again I hear some people give a historical answer: "Separation of church and state has always been a fundamental conviction of Protestantism." Clearly, this is an oversimplification if not an outright misrepresentation of church history. But for some people it is sufficient cause to decide that the church must limit its activities to otherworldly concerns. Contemporary American Protestants may feel that they have good reason to espouse the pragmatic principle of separation of church and state. But that decision hardly precludes a concern about the society in which the church lives. Even Protestantism outside state churches has a long heritage of concern for the "worldly" aspects of life and a sense of responsibility for peace and justice in the nation. Why has this aspect of tradition been so controversial and so hard to keep alive in some circles? I suspect that the problem stems partly from the contemporary American Protestant incomprehension of a "parish." Those who have grown up in "gathered" or "voluntary" churches do not grasp the interconnectedness of all the citizens of a medieval or Reformation community or the church's sense of responsibility for all of life in such a community. Unfortunately, some of today's Protestants who remember warmly those days of the interconnectedness of church and state have forgotten its damage to personal liberty and freedom of conscience. Our congregations seem to remember the tradition only selectively. One elder chairing a church-and-society commission that continually

asked whether it was appropriate for a congregation in our tradition to
become involved in social action proposed that the group read W. Fred
Graham's book on Calvin's involvement in the Reformation's restructuring of
the life of the city of Geneva.[1] Becoming acquainted with the historical
material proved to be a useful catalyst for the group's own decision about
what was appropriate for that congregation to do in the community and the
reasons for its decision.

   Still another set of questions concerns theological unity or uniformity in
the church. Does it matter whether everyone in a congregation agrees in
theology? What is the role of the historic confessions for those living in an age
in which the worldview has profoundly changed? These questions provoke
lively debate in some neighboring congregations as a result of a case currently in church courts arising from opposition to a particular minister's
understanding of the Nicene Creed. The complainants seem to believe that
interpreting a creed or confession "literally" is necessary in order to preserve
the tradition faithfully. In our denomination, the church courts that must
decide the case are made up of ministers and ruling elders. The latter are
ordained church officers, of whom only a few have had seminary training. Yet
in this precise juridical sense, as well as in a more general sense, the
responsibility of deciding how the theological tradition is to be understood
and taught is placed in their hands as well as those of the ministers. Custom
and church law stress the importance of teaching the tradition to the whole
congregation, and especially to those who serve as church officers. Yet lay
people tell me over and over again that no one has ever tried to help them
understand the historical context of the ancient and Reformation creeds.
Even some lay people who have begun to understand critical methods of
biblical study, who are learning to ask what point the biblical author is trying
to make in a particular social, intellectual, and religious context, and who ask
about the language used, do not yet see that they must approach historic
creedal statements in a similar fashion. The communication of historical
method to those who must deal with historical materials in the context of
contemporary church life is therefore urgently needed. Congregations are
asking general questions about the concept of an authoritative tradition of
theology: Does "heresy" have any meaning today? Can one hold to freedom
of conscience and still consider Scripture and/or historic confessions authoritative? Is a theological defense of racism heresy, as the World Alliance of
Reformed Churches has declared? What about a defense of women's subordination? These questions grow out of concrete experiences and require
some knowledge of history if one is to answer responsibly.

   I still hear in Protestant churches many questions about the role of
women. Some are questions growing out of the awareness of Catholic and

---

[1] W. Fred Graham, *The Constructive Revolutionary: John Calvin and His Socio-Economic
Impact* (Richmond: John Knox Press, 1971).

Orthodox women's struggle for access to ordained office and responsible decision-making positions. Some come from the Protestants' increasing sensitivity to their own failure to produce the equality for women that most Protestant churches have promised. Many in the churches realize that there are conflicting views today of the history of women in the church: The traditional view regards the subordination of women as the church's universal historical experience and also as normative. At least one of the other views is that the subordination of women, however widely practiced, is a perversion of authentic tradition and in conflict with at least some historical experience in the church's life. Unfortunately, more of today's ministers attended seminary when no women's history was included in the seminary curriculum and thus they know little about the roles of real historical women in the church. Even if such ministers do support equal roles for women today on the basis of their ethical principles, they are not prepared to deal with the historical questions that underlie much feminist theological work in the church. Why is there so much difference between the place of women in the New Testament church and in the medieval church? Why should the church's male leadership have felt the need to suppress the stories of women in the early church and to restrict women's leadership? Why did the Reformers not give women the full freedom that the priesthood of all believers seems to imply? What historical evidence do we have of women's religious experience? Why has so little of the history of women in the church found its way into post-Enlightenment seminary lectures and textbooks? Many laywomen are reading the works of feminist biblical scholars and historians such as Elisabeth Schuessler Fiorenza, Rosemary Ruether, and Bernadette Brooten that raise questions about the history of women in the church. They are eager to discuss these new insights with theologically trained people. Women pastors are usually happy to do so. But I have seen little evidence that the male pastors of local congregations are reading feminist theology and history. In fact, the communications gap between women who read theology and male pastors seems to be growing. The reluctance of male pastors to discuss these issues with women parishioners is unfortunately reinforcing the tendency of many male parishioners to see feminist issues as irrelevant to the church at large.

Ecumenical concerns are alive in the congregations with which I work. Church members feel that it is appropriate to be cordial to other churches, that it is natural and, indeed, necessary to cooperate on social-action projects, and that it is essential to engage in mutual-aid enterprises both in this country and abroad. Most would, I think, add that it is important to know something about the theology and practice of other churches, but many deem it rude or impolite to ask direct questions of members of other churches about their distinctive thought and practice. There seems to be relatively little sense of urgency about faith-and-order matters. Some laypersons, however, have participated for several years in Lenten living-room dialogues between Catholics and Protestants. This year a study group was organized from members of a Lutheran and a Presbyterian congregation to study the report of the North American Lutheran-Reformed bilateral dialogue dealing with intercommunion between the two groups. Several interdenominational groups and workshops were established to focus on the WCC Lima document on baptism, eucharist, and ministry. When such a format permits face-to-face ecumenical discussion, the lay people's interest in faith-and-order matters becomes evident. Participants regularly express the need for historical background to understand the reasons for denominations' divisions and estrangement. Once congregations begin such faith-and-order discussions, the level of historical awareness and the sense of urgency in these questions rise noticeably.

There is also some concern about anti-Semitism. One congregation responded to the vandalism of a Jewish newspaper-owner's office by beginning an annual weekend of exchange with the nearest synagogue. The experience of worshiping in each other's congregations raised many theological and historical questions. As the members of the two congregations began to get acquainted, the question of the reasons for Christian anti-Semitism became more urgent. Many members of the Christian congregation had assumed that Hitler invented anti-Semitism. Members of the Jewish congregation, however, were more aware of the long history of Christian anti-Semitism. Learning about the positive and negative relations of Christians and Jews through history was both painful and instructive for the Christian congregation.

Usually congregations' first request regarding church history, often arising from sheer curiosity, is for biography: For example, they are interested in learning more about Augustine, the various reformers, and women in the history of the church. They want to hear stories of the past. But one who knows something about church history can help a congregation also learn to draw on history to answer questions, explain present faith and practice, provide options and models from which to choose, cope positively with change, and set priorities for action.

An effective way of encouraging lay people to see the usefulness of asking historical questions is to begin with their own congregation. By discussing what sorts of sources are available to them to explain how the congregation came to be what it is, they will learn the various sources that historians actually use. They can explore the history of the church buildings, the reasons for the style of architecture, the pattern of liturgy, the periods of growth and retrenchment in the congregation and their relation to the life of the broader community, the ethnic backgrounds of the church's members, and the nature of church leadership. They will quickly see that many of their questions cannot be answered from written documents, even when those questions concern current issues. The attempt to understand their own congregations' history may stimulate some oral history efforts and perhaps other changes in the ways that they keep their records. It may also raise many helpful questions about the congregation's mission, priorities, and methods, as well as about its roots.

The Impact of Congregations on Seminary Teaching of Church History

Survey Courses

Let us consider the content of the first semester of church history, usually including the early, medieval and Reformation periods. Traditionally the required courses have been built around familiar church-history textbooks. These courses are thus long on popes and councils, institutions like monasticism, church and state, and major theologians; they are short on the history of the laity, especially women's history, the history of congregational life, worship, popular religion, and spirituality. They usually move directly from the Middle East to Europe, rarely venturing south of Alexandria. Such a format does not address directly the sorts of questions I have described as important to the congregational life I know. Even though the topics of such a course are certainly relevant to the contemporary church, students find the relevance difficult to grasp. Because many students may not take any other courses on the history of the church before 1600, the materials that the required course uses should enable the students to see easily the relevance of history to the life of the congregations they will serve.

Given the shortness of a single semester, hard choices must be made. There always will be a need for some sort of narrative survey of general developments, especially as few of today's students have acquired an overall view of even Western Christianity in their undergraduate programs. But beyond this orientation is needed a close reading of primary sources to which seminarians can relate as they gain skill in using historical methods and insights for their professional work. If they become comfortable working with historical materials, they presumably will broaden their knowledge through independent reading over their years as pastors.

When the institution in which I was teaching a few years ago first began to move toward basic required courses, I chose the history of worship as the focus of the first church history course. For some years I had been teaching an elective course on the history of worship and ecclesiology and had found these topics suitable to introductory work. Even those students with the worst cases of "history anxiety" could see the relevance of these topics to parish work. By holding together worship and the doctrine of the church, the instructor can avoid the tendency to make liturgics too technical and at the same time can demonstrate the connection between theology and practice. This model has now been built into the required course. Thompson's paperback collection of Western liturgical texts makes available in translation ten liturgies from before 1600.[2] Supplementing this reading with primary sources for related theological issues provides a foundation for later work in

---

[2] Bard Thompson, *Liturgies of the Western Church* (Philadelphia: Fortress Press, 1980).

systematic theology; and the liturgical material provides a base on which a later course in preparing and leading worship services can build.

What related theological issues are included? The course's ecclesiological aspect brings students into dialogue with Irenaeus and Cyprian on the nature of the episcopacy and the doctrine of apostolic succession, with medieval writers on mariology and the cult of the saints, with Luther on the priesthood of all believers and the Anabaptists on the gathered church. To understand the liturgical texts, the students must explore eucharistic theology through the entire historical period, and they will often be startled at the way these two sorts of texts illuminate each other. Such a course must also cover the development of christology and the creeds in relation to communion with Christ in the eucharist and excommunication and also the development of the other sacraments. Beginning with worship, then, the instructor can lead the students from a familiar aspect of congregational life to most of the classical theological topics, seeing them in relation to changing patterns of Christian life—in particular, historical contexts—rather than as theological abstractions. The students will also become familiar with some of the basic issues in ecumenical conversation, especially if the instructor adds to Thompson's collection the Liturgy of St. John Chrysostom of the Eastern church.

A focus on worship also leads the instructor to deal with the changing understanding of the roles of the minister and the laity. Many materials on the history of the clergy are readily available, but those on the history of the laity are more difficult to find. Weber's study of the laity is a useful starting place, although it is now out of print.[3] The many newer social-history studies bring helpful perspectives on the life and thought of lay people. One example is the Ladurie study of Montaillou. Bishop Fournier of Pamier, later Avignon Pope Benedict XII, conducted an episcopal inquisition in the village of Montaillou in the Pyrenees between 1318 and 1325 in an effort to stamp out the last of the Cathar heresy. Of the ninety-four people interviewed extensively by the bishop, most were ordinary people like peasants and shopkeepers, and of of these, forty-eight were women. Ladurie has drawn from the extensive documentation of the interviews a fascinating picture of a mountain village and its religious life, in which one can see the way in which "heresy" and "orthodoxy" are interwoven in the lives of simple people.[4] Such a view is a helpful corrective to the common impression that students receive from textbooks that once a council defines heresy, the heresy instantly disappears. Other approaches to the history of the laity are available, for example, studies on the role of the laity in developing medieval

[3] Hans-Reudi Weber, *The Layman in Christian History* (Philadelphia: Westminster Press, 1963).

[4] Emmanuel LeRoy Ladurie, *Montaillou: The Promised Land of Error*, trans. Barbara Bray (New York: Braziller, 1978), esp. vii–xvii and chap. 19.

legends of miracles.[5] A more institutional role can be seen in the parishioners' increased responsibility for maintining church buildings and properties in late medieval England,[6] related to the development of the office of churchwarden.

Perhaps most important for instructors who wish to incorporate the history of the laity into the curriculum is to make a habit of noticing the perspective of the laity in familiar documents. For example, "The Pilgrimage of Egeria" has been known for a century to students of liturgy as a rare witness to the early celebration of Easter week in Jerusalem. Egeria, apparently a woman of some standing in society, visited Jerusalem, Mount Sinai, the shrine of Saint Thekla, and other holy places in the fourth or fifth century and wrote a detailed account of her experiences to women friends who were deeply interested in religious matters. In her account of the elaborate liturgical observances of Holy Week in Jerusalem, she tells of joining the throngs of lay people visiting the holy places and describes the experience from their point of view. When the story of Jesus' arrest is read to the worshipers, " . . . there is such moaning and groaning with weeping among the people that they can be heard by all the people of the city."[7] As the crowds walk from one holy site to another for devotional services, singing hymns as the dawn breaks after their all-night vigil, the bishop comforts the people "because they have labored the whole night long and they are to work this whole day."[8] Worship is the people's "labor," work that they share with their bishop. There is nothing passive about the worshipers that Egeria describes. She also outlines the teaching of the catechumens being prepared for baptism on Easter eve. After inscription before the first day of Lent and inquiry by the bishop about their character, they are exorcised daily, early in the morning.

> Immediately afterwards, the bishop's chair is placed in the Martyrium, the great church, and all who are to be baptized sit in a circle around the bishop, men as well as women, while the fathers and the mothers stand there. All of the people who wish to hear may come in and sit down, if they are of the faithful.[9]

---

[5] For example, Ronald C. Finucane, *Miracles and Pilgrims: Popular Beliefs in Medieval England* (Totowa, N.J.: Rowman and Littlefield, 1977), chap. 9.

[6] Colin Platt, *The Parish Churches of Medieval England* (London: Secker & Warburg, 1981), chap. 5.

[7] Patricia Wilson-Kastner, G. Ronald Kastner, Ann Millin, Rosemary Rader, and Jeremiah Reedy, *A Lost Tradition: Women Writers of the Early Church* (Washington, D.C.: University Press of America, 1981), 121.

[8] Wilson-Kastner et al., 121; cf. 127.

[9] Wilson-Kastner et al., 129.

For five weeks the bishop teaches the Scriptures and then the Symbol. Egeria explains to her "ladies and sisters" that "the faithful who have come in to hear the catechesis which is explained by the bishop raise their voices [in questioning] more than when the bishop sits and preaches [in church] about each of the things being explained."[10] Egeria's description of the congregational setting for the "catechetical orations" that have come down to us from bishops of the period adds a valuable perspective. She adds a further unusual detail in explaining that the congregation is multilingual and that great efforts are made to be sure that everyone understands whatever is said. The bishop always speaks in Greek, but a presbyter always stands by him to translate into Syriac for those who do not understand Greek. If Latin-speaking persons are present who understand neither Greek nor Syriac, "in order that they might not be left in the dark, all is explained to them because there are brothers and sisters who speak both Greek and Latin who can explain it to them in Latin."[11]

Egeria suggests that worship and education are the work of the whole community, not just of the clergy. This insight can simply be a corrective to overly narrow descriptions of the history of church life. But it can also point to a theological imperative to refocus our attention on the congregation. Those who believe that the whole church has been called to ministry have a special obligation to search for and present whatever evidence may be available for the community's involvement in such ministries as evangelism, pastoral nurture, and care of the poor and suffering. Such a perspective may lead to the use of new sorts of sources and also new insights into well-known sources. Here theological motivation will encourage questions about the focus of the historical tradition on the clergy and thus will permit new conclusions. But it must not be allowed to dictate unfairly the historian's conclusions on the basis of the evidence.

The use of Egeria's writings also illustrates the fact that it is possible, if not always easy, to find women's writings in English translation from the period before 1600 that contribute significantly to the study of the topic at hand. The concern of women clergy and laywomen in the congregations to learn about their foremothers makes it essential that materials by women and concerning women in the church be regularly included in all course reading lists. They need to be part of the theological education of male as well as female pastors.

My description of the congregations that have shaped my outlook mentioned that several are culturally Asian and Hispanic, as are many of my seminary students. Other students come from Africa and the Pacific islands. Although my own formal training in church history included nothing about Asian, African, or Latin American church history, my colleagues in the

---

[10] Wilson-Kastner et al., 129.
[11] Wilson-Kastner et al., 130.

congregations and my students have helped me realize the need to educate myself as well as my students in this area. All seminarians need to develop their global consciousness while studying history. In a basic survey course, the instructor can call attention to the expansion of Christianity not only in the Mediterranean area and northern Europe but also, during the early and medieval periods, in Africa, India, and the Far East. While studying the Catholic Reformation, for example, students can explore the differences between the approaches of the Franciscans in Latin America and the Jesuits in Asia to the indigenous cultures. Primary source material is now available in English on Bartolomé de las Casas and his struggles to protect the rights of native Americans in the Caribbean.[12] Las Casas is an increasingly important figure in both Catholic and Protestant Hispanic discussion of the period but is seldom included in Protestant curricula.

The congregations have also reinforced my perception of the importance of including material on the interaction of Christianity with postbiblical Judaism and the interaction of Western Christianity with Eastern orthodoxy.

All these things cannot be done in depth in a single basic course. But one can lay foundations and establish expectations that a well-trained pastor will continue to learn about such topics.

Specialized Courses

In a course setting where one has the leisure to work in greater depth, it is useful to explore the life of the church in a particular locality, looking at the social and economic setting, the church institutions, the clergy and the lay people, and the changing religious life and thought. Congregational life can be seen in a rich context in sixteenth-century Strasbourg, for example, on the basis of recent, complementary studies.

Miriam Chrisman has provided a general study of the Strasbourg Reformation and also two specialized volumes devoted to books being read and printed in Strasbourg during the Reformation period.[13] Some of these books were clearly intended for lay people, others, for clergy. Church-and-state issues focusing on the role of the laity can be discussed using the studies of Thomas A. Brady[14] and Lorna Jane Abray.[15] Several studies deal with

[12] Bartolomé de las Casas, *In Defense of the Indians*, ed. Stafford Poole (DeKalb: Northern Illinois University Press, 1974); Juan Friede, ed., *Bartolomé de las Casas in History* (DeKalb: Northern Illinois University Press, 1971).

[13] Miriam Usher Chrisman, *Strasbourg and the Reform: A Study in the Process of Change* (New Haven, Conn.: Yale University Press, 1967); Miriam Usher Chrisman, *Lay Culture, Learned Culture: Books and Social Change in Strasbourg, 1480–1599* (New Haven, Conn.: Yale University Press, 1982); Miriam Usher Chrisman, *Bibliography of Strasbourg Imprints, 1480–1599* (New Haven, Conn.: Yale University Press, 1982).

[14] Thomas A. Brady, Jr., *Ruling Class, Regime and Reformation at Strasbourg, 1520–1555* (Leiden: Brill, 1978).

[15] Lorna Jane Abray, *The People's Reformation: Magistrates, Clergy, and Commons in Strasbourg 1500–1598* (Ithaca, N.Y.: Cornell University Press, 1985).

worship, sacramental life, and pastoral care in the city during the Reformation, especially those by René Bornert,[16] Hughes Oliphant Old,[17] W. D. Maxwell,[18] and François Wendel.[19] Bornert discusses the sacraments, discipline, marriage, the ministry and ordination, visits to the ill, and funerals. Old and Maxwell focus on public worship. Wendel describes the structures of church life and marriage. English translations are available of Bucer's Strasbourg liturgy[20] and some of his writings about the sacraments and pastoral care.[21] Chrisman discusses in an article the place of women in the Reformation,[22] and Roland Bainton contributes brief biographies of two significant wives of Strasbourg pastors, Katherine Zell and Wibrandis Rosenblatt.[23] The diversity of theological points of view in Strasbourg during the Reformation can be seen in the numerous studies of Bucer,[24] Capito,[25] and Vermigli.[26] Additional insight into this theological ferment is provided by Franklin Littell's translation of the transcript of a public debate between Bucer and a local Anabaptist leader,[27] and also by George Williams's[28] and Willem Balke's[29] discussions of radical reformers in the area.

If seminaries were to consider seriously a focus on the congregation,

[16] René Bornert, *La Réforme Protestante du Culte à Strasbourg au XVIe Siècle (1523–1598)* (Leiden: Brill, 1981).

[17] Hughes Oliphant Old, *The Patristic Roots of Reformed Worship* (Zürich: Theologischer Verlag, 1975), 80–92, 119–130; Hughes Oliphant Old, "Daily Prayer in the Reformed Church of Strasbourg, 1525–1530," *Worship* 52 (1978): 121–138.

[18] W. D. Maxwell, *John Knox's Genevan Service Book, 1556* (Edinburgh: s. n., 1931).

[19] François Wendel, *L'Eglise de Strasbourg, sa constitution et son organisation, 1532–1535* (Paris: Presses universitaires de France, 1942); François Wendel, *Le mariage à Strasbourg à l'époque de la réforme, 1520–1692* (Strasbourg: Imprimerie Alascienne, 1928).

[20] "Martin Bucer, The Strassburg Liturgy" in Thompson, chap. 6.

[21] Martin Bucer, *Common Places of Martin Bucer*, trans. and ed. D. F. Wright (Appleford, England: Sutton Courtenay Press, 1972), is an anthology of Bucer's theological and pastoral writings.

[22] Miriam Usher Chrisman, "Women and the Reformation in Strasbourg, 1490–1530," *Archiv für Reformationsgeschichte* 63 (1972): 141–168.

[23] Roland Bainton, *Women of the Reformation in Germany and Italy* (Minneapolis: Augsburg Publishing House, 1971), chaps. 3, 4, on Katherine Zell and Wibrandis Rosenblatt.

[24] For example, W. P. Stephens, *The Holy Spirit in the Theology of Martin Bucer* (Cambridge, England: Cambridge University Press, 1970); Basil Hall, "Diakonia in Martin Butzer," in *Service in Christ*, ed. James I. McCord and T. H. L. Parker (Grand Rapids, Mich.: Eerdmans, 1966), 89–100.

[25] James M. Kittelson, *Wolfgang Capito: from Humanist to Reformer* (Leiden: Brill, 1975).

[26] John Patrick Donnelly, *Calvinism and Scholasticism in Vermigli's Doctrine of Man and Grace* (Leiden: Brill, 1976).

[27] Franklin H. Littell, "New Light on Butzer's Significance," in *Reformation Studies: Essays in Honor of Roland H. Bainton*, ed. Franklin H. Littel (Richmond: John Knox Press, 1962), 145–167.

[28] George H. Williams, *The Radical Reformation* (Philadelphia: Westminster Press, 1962), chap. X.

[29] Willem Balke, *Calvin and the Anabaptist Radicals*, trans. William Heynen (Grand Rapids, Mich.: Eerdmans, 1981), chap. V.

they would attempt such revisions in their course offerings. If they were very serious, they would require prospective students to have been adult members of congregations for at least two years, carrying some responsibility for leadership there as a layperson. This would be different from having grown up in a congregation and relating to a minister as a child; it would also be different from trying out ministerial roles in field work in a congregation. Those who as adults have been working members of a congregation seem to have greater respect for the laity and a more realistic understanding of how congregations really function. There is an identification with the congregation from within.

Recently a first-year student, a woman who has been deeply engaged in congregational life as an adult for probably twenty years, came to ask some very probing questions about the BEM document. When I asked why she had been studying it, she replied, "My congregation wants to understand it, and I have so little background in these matters. I've been reading all I can find about it so I can help my congregation grasp what it is saying and think about the issues it raises. We need to understand!" She would understand very well my proposals for studying church history!

THE CONGREGATION AND NEW TESTAMENT STUDIES

Carl R. Holladay

Various proposals have been made that would give new prominence to the congregation in theological education. If some such proposal were adopted, what difference might it make for the field of New Testament, both for research and teaching?

First, with respect to research on the New Testament conducted in the professional guilds, what agenda(s) would be created? What new directions of research would emerge? What already established directions of research would be redirected, modified, and perhaps terminated? What current directions of research would most naturally inform and enhance the study of the congregation? What is already being done that would provide resources or perspectives useful to the field of congregational studies? What, in brief, would be the impact of such a shift on the current research on the New Testament and Christian origins?

Second, with respect to teaching, how would the way in which the New Testament is taught in a seminary curriculum be affected by this shift? How would it change the way in which seminary students are introduced to the study of the New Testament? What would a syllabus for a New Testament Introduction course look like? How would courses in particular books be taught? How would the skills normally learned in New Testament courses, notably exegesis, be taught and learned? What, in brief, would be the impact of such a shift on the teaching of the New Testament and Christian origins?

New Testament Research: A Historical Overview

Before attempting to determine the possible impact of a congregational agenda on New Testament research, we need a historical overview within which we can assess the prospects.

The effect of the rise of historical consciousness in the modern period is well known. Like theological studies in general, the agenda for biblical studies has been largely set by the historical paradigm, with the historical-critical method becoming the predominant tool. Even though the rise and development of historical criticism are still being assessed and the overall value of its contributions is now being seriously questioned,[1] at least it has resulted in a drive for historical concreteness that bodes well for congregational studies. It might even be suggested that under the impulse of historical criticism, New Testament scholars have worked with an increasingly concrete notion of the church. That is, their questions have driven them to think more and more concretely about local Christian communities—their geographical location, their historical and social milieus, the dynamics of their relationship with their social culture, the religious traditions on which they draw and that they themselves form and transmit, and various aspects of their life of faith, including their worship, preaching, and catechesis. To the degree that we have been able to reconstruct the historical particularities of early Christian congregations, our understanding of the New Testament writings themselves has shifted.

This increasingly particular form of historical reconstruction begins at least as early as F. C. Baur, for whom the fundamental reconstructive categories for studying the New Testament were Pauline and Petrine Christianity—two streams of tradition alongside which the New Testament writings could be divided and through which they could be interpreted.[2] Even when analyzing the particular situation at Corinth, these were the categories used. In the early twentieth century, the fundamental reconstructive categories on which much New Testament work was done were *Palestinian Christianity*, otherwise designated as *Jewish Christianity*, and *non-Palestinian Christianity*, otherwise designated as *Hellenistic* or *Gentile Christianity*. This was certainly the scheme that informed R. Bultmann's *History of the Synoptic Tradition* and *Theology of the New Testament*, and his work was typical of many others of the period.[3] As form criticism developed in the hands of its most creative practitioners, most notably Dibelius, it became clear that a more historically concrete set of categories was needed to account for the formation and development of the Gospels tradition. Already in Dibelius's *From Tradition to Gospel* these categories begin to emerge, as he frequently speaks of the concrete situations in Christian congregations or

---

[1] Cf. F. Hahn, *Historical Investigation and New Testament Faith: Two Essays* (Philadelphia: Fortress Press, 1983), esp. 13–33; also N. R. Peterson, *Literary Criticism for New Testament Critics*, Guides to Biblical Scholarship (Philadelphia: Fortress Press, 1978), esp. 9–23.

[2] F. C. Baur, "Die Christuspartei in der korinthischen Gemeinde, der Gegensatz des petrinischen und paulinischen Christenthums in der altesten Kirche, der Apostel Petrus in Rom," *Tuebinger Zeitschrift fuer Theologie* 4 (1831): 61–206; cf. also H. Koester, "New Testament Introduction: A Critique of a Discipline," in *Christianity, Judaism, and Other Greco-Roman Cults. Part I: New Testament*, ed. J. Neusner (Leiden: Brill, 1979), 1–20, esp. 2–3.

[3] Even though R. Bultmann, *History of the Synoptic Tradition*, rev. ed. (New York: Harper & Row, 1963), 1–7, formulates his approach to form criticism recognizing the important role of the early Christian community in creating and shaping the tradition, the fundamental categories that inform his analytical work are already indicated in his statement of purpose: "Hence an essential part of my inquiry concerns the one chief problem of primitive Christianity, the relationship of the primitive Palestinian and Hellenistic Christianity" (5).

communities within which certain traditions regarding Jesus originated and developed.[4] With the emergence of the *Sitz im Leben* as an accepted heuristic category, form critics learned to think more and more of the actual situation of a local community of faith as the generative matrix of early Christian traditions. The results, for the most part, were only hypothetical. The congregations could be imagined only because of the nature of the Gospels traditions. Unlike the Epistles, none of the Gospels was explicitly addressed to a local church. For that matter, there were only occasional references to what might be construed as congregational settings, and these were indirect at best.

With the onset and development of redaction criticism, the notion of church gained even greater concreteness as a category for New Testament studies. Form criticism succeeded in demonstrating that the churches, in some sense, played a formative, indeed a creative, role in the development of the Gospels tradition, but they remained largely faceless and undifferentiated, except when lumped together under the general rubric of Palestinian churches/Christianity or Gentile churches/Christianity. The redaction critics achieved greater specificity in their insistence that the Gospels be seen as the consciously composed works of individual evangelists or theologians, and when such individual authorship was inconceivable, as works reflecting the theological outlook of a community of faith. In any case, the notion of church achieved greater concreteness as redaction critics began to speak of the Matthean church/churches or community or, more generally, Matthean Christianity.[5] With greater or lesser degrees of specificity, the Markan, Lukan, and Johannine churches were envisioned as the loci within which

---

[4] M. Dibelius, *From Tradition to Gospel* (Cambridge, England: James Clark & Co., 1971), in contrast with Bultmann's analytical method, uses a "constructive method which attempts to include the conditions and activities of life of the first Christian Churches" (10). Dibelius's analysis of the synoptic tradition is consistently informed by a concrete notion of the individual Christian community, and this represents one of the most important features distinguishing it from Bultmann's work. Indeed, it might be said that Dibelius operates with a much more historically concrete understanding of congregation than does Bultmann. Typical is Dibelius's analysis of Mark 2:23–28, in which he accounts for the concluding words of the pericope, "so the Son of Man is Lord even of the Sabbath": "The problem is solved much more simply if we see even in the final words a *saying from a sermon*, i.e. the congregation is referred to the answer of Jesus, and thereby its hearers could see that the Son of Man, this Jesus, is also Lord of the Sabbath (cf. also Mark 10:45)" (65). Interestingly enough, in the handbook on form criticism by R. Bultmann and K. Kundsin, *Form Criticism: Two Essays on New Testament Research* (New York: Harper Torchbooks, 1962), the essay by Kundsin, though reflecting the basic categories with which Bultmann worked (cf. 84–85 and the outline of the essay), nevertheless reflects a view of the ancient Christian community nearly as concrete and well defined as that of Dibelius; 87–88, 143–144.

[5] A redaction critical approach is consistently followed by E. Schweizer in his commentaries on the synoptic Gospels. Especially in *The Good News According to Matthew* (Atlanta: John Knox Press, 1975) does a clearly etched portrait of the Matthean community emerge; cf. 17; also 178–186, where the extent of specificity is seen in the excursus "Prophets, Wise Men, Teachers, and the Righteous in the Matthean Community."

their traditions regarding Jesus were preserved and reached their final form, either as the creators and preservers of those traditions or as those for whom such traditions were created and preserved and to whom they were addressed in the final form of the respective Gospels. So well have such categories as Johannine Christianity or Pauline Christianity served the needs of New Testament scholarship that they have become fundamental to the way we read the New Testament and reconstruct the history of early Christianity.

Even though redaction criticism succeeded in producing a more historically concrete understanding of the churches to and for whom the Gospels were written, it was still not altogether clear to what extent we could or should think of them as local congregations. In the case of Johannine Christianity, it seems highly likely that we should envision local congregations within a defined geographical area, probably Asia Minor, as representing this theological outlook. This judgment is possible, however, because we possess three epistles to be read along with the Fourth Gospel, a form of methodological control not available to us with the synoptic Gospels. Even so, the main way of providing greater delineation to these churches from reading the Gospels is not so much by referring to the churches themselves but by reconstructing the theological viewpoint of the evangelist as expressed in the Gospels and assuming that this viewpoint is in some sense expressive of the church(es) associated with the Gospels, as an originator, preserver, and transmitter of the tradition or as a recipient/addressee.

It was at this juncture that New Testament scholarship met a methodological impasse. Once the Gospels were seen as the work of creative theologians addressing churches with clearly defined needs, it was only a short step to begin reconstructing the theological profile not only of the churches to whom the Gospels were addressed but also of churches with a conflicting or opposing theological outlook. The Gospels now began to be used as windows through which to view churches with heretical theologies. It then became clear that such historical reconstruction was methodologically dubious: first reading the Gospels to reconstruct the theology of the author/evangelist, coordinating that with a church or group of churches seen as the evangelist's community, then reconstructing the theology of the opposition, and coordinating that with a church or group of churches, perhaps as seen through the text of the Gospels themselves or as alluded to or reconstructed from some other New Testament writing, such as 2 Corinthians.

At this stage, scholars began to wonder whether the text was being overly manipulated.[6] Not surprisingly, the focus shifted as New Testament scholars became more fascinated with literary questions. As the literary

---

[6]Cf. L. T. Johnson, "On Finding the Lukan Community: A Cautious Cautionary Essay," in *Society of Biblical Literature 1979 Seminar Papers* (Missoula, Mont.: Scholars Press, 1979), 87–100.

criticism of the New Testament, especially as influenced by the New Criticism, has flourished, the historical realities behind the Gospels, whether conceived in the broadest possible terms such as Palestinian Christianity and Gentile Christianity or in more narrowly defined, concrete terms such as Matthean Christianity, are nevertheless viewed in some sense as churches. The real question is whether the material at our disposal allows us to become much more historically specific than this in defining these churches.[7] Whatever the case, it is nevertheless still arguable that the impulse of historical criticism as it has come to be applied to the New Testament has been to push for historical concreteness, and one way in which this has been done is for New Testament scholars to develop an understanding of church that moves closer and closer to that of the local church or congregation.

Current Directions in New Testament Research and Their Relation to Congregational Studies

If, as I have argued, historical criticism helped give New Testament scholars a great consciousness of the local church, indeed enabled them to develop a more historically concrete understanding of the church that moves toward the local congregation, we should assess some of the current mainstreams of New Testament study to determine whether similar results are likely.

1. *Social history.* The renewed interest in appropriating the theoretical framework and investigative methods of the social sciences for New Testament research bodes well for congregational studies.[8] Even though this recent trend in New Testament study has roots at least as early as Shirley Jackson Case, its newer version can be construed as in direct continuity with the historical critical study of the New Testament. Its aim is still history, but history in a different sense. The enterprise is variously designated as *social* or *sociological,* but in either case its purpose is to investigate the social

---

[7] That this can be done convincingly is suggested by the work of R. E. Brown, especially *The Community of the Beloved Disciple* (New York: Paulist Press, 1978); *The Churches the Apostles Left Behind* (New York: Paulist Press, 1984); "New Testament Background for the Concept of Local Church," *Proceedings of Catholic Theological Society of America* 36 (1981): 1–14. This latter article provides many of the New Testament data pertaining to the concept of the local church and pushes for even more imaginatively construed profiles of New Testament congregations, suggesting various forms of Pauline communities, post-Pauline communities, Johannine communities, communities related to the Gospel of Matthew, the Epistles of 1 Peter and James, and to major geographical centers.

[8] Cf. esp. J. G. Gager, *Kingdom and Community: The Social World of Early Christianity* (Englewood Cliffs, N.J.: Prentice-Hall, 1975); G. Theissen, *The Social Setting of Pauline Christianity* (Edinburgh: T. & T. Clark, 1982); W. Meeks, *The First Urban Christians: The Social World of the Apostle Paul* (New Haven, Conn.: Yale University Press, 1983); A. J. Malherbe, *Social Aspects of Early Christianity,* 2nd ed. (Philadelphia: Fortress Press, 1983), esp. the extensive bibliography, 113–122.

history of early Christianity. The New Testament still remains a central focus, but there is less concern to reconstruct the history of early Christianity as traditionally conceived or the history of early Christian traditions, as was the case with form and redaction criticism. Rather, the task is to uncover the social reality, or the social world, of early Christianity, and so far this has meant, among other things, a sociological analysis of early Christian communities.

For congregational studies, one of the most beneficial results of this study has been the work done on Pauline Christianity in general, and on Christianity at Corinth in particular.[9] We can see the unique value of the New Testament writings as sources for investigating the internal dynamics of early Christian communities, at least when compared with the sources available to us for studying other ancient religious communities.[10] In the case of the church at Corinth, the sources for making a sociological analysis of an ancient Christian congregation are quite rich and through careful study have yielded richly textured reconstructions of this local church. Such reconstructions are providing valuable new perspectives for understanding the New Testament text, as well as for illuminating the possibilities and limitations of New Testament theology.

2. *Literary approaches.* With the increasing interest in applying literary perspectives to the study of the New Testament text, congregational studies stand to benefit in a different way.[11] To be sure, current literary approaches to the New Testament show less interest in the congregation, conceptual or empirical, than does the more traditional approach. Its emphasis lies more in the message woven into the text, and the literary structures through which it is mediated, than with what can be reconstructed from the text. The focus is on literary themes, literary forms, and their functions, especially narrative. Narrative elements of the Gospels have long been noted, as have the narrative elements of smaller units such as parables. Other studies have investigated the narrative structure and substructure of other parts of the New Testament, including the letters of Paul.

It may well be that this heightened interest in the narrative elements of the New Testament will both inform and be informed by those initiatives in congregational studies that seek to explore the relationship between congregations and their stories.[12] If empirical studies of modern congregations

---

[9]Corinth is the primary focus of Theissen's essays in *Social Setting* and also figures prominently in the work of Malherbe and Meeks.

[10]This is especially emphasized by E. A. Judge, *The Social Pattern of Christian Groups in the First Century* (London: Tyndale House, 1960).

[11]An introduction to the already extensive literature is provided by J. H. Gottcent, *The Bible As Literature: A Selective Bibliography* (Boston: G. K. Hall, 1979); also D. Robertson, *The Old Testament and the Literary Critic* (Philadelphia: Fortress Press, 1977).

[12]Cf. J. F. Hopewell, "The Jovial Church: Narratives in Local Church Life," in *Building Effective Ministry: Theory and Practice in the Local Church*, ed. Carl S. Dudley (San Francisco: Harper & Row, 1983), 68–83.

succeed in demonstrating that individual congregations can be analyzed in terms of the stories that they themselves relate, as well as the mythic structures that they embody, this in itself may provide important clues to understanding the New Testament materials. This may lead in turn to an inquiry into the relationship between the form of the congregation and the form of its story, between social-historical form and narrative form. If for example, a congregation construes reality through the use of an apocalyptic story, so that its social definition may be said to be apocalyptic, how does this empirical congregational entity relate to the story it tells? Studies of New Testament materials have already explored the relationship between sectarian forms of community and the types of myth that give rise to and inform them.[13] Among other things, this provides a useful way of exploring the dynamics of conflict, as when one form of community with a myth that reinforces its identity begins to be exposed to and absorb another myth that questions this form and perhaps even requires its abandonment.

As the literary study of the New Testament progresses, we may expect to learn even more about the form and function of the New Testament's various literary genres and subgenres. As we do, and as we explore the possible correlations between the forms of community and the forms of literature used in those communities, we may discover even more about the nature of Christian congregations. Conversely, the continued study of modern congregations in terms of their own narratives—accompanied by the effort to determine the various types of stories that congregations tell and by which they define themselves—may enrich our understanding of the relationship between the congregational form and the congregational story and, in turn, enable us to see aspects of the New Testament heretofore invisible.

3. *Structuralist studies.* It remains to be seen whether structuralism will become a firmly established method or perspective for interpreting the New Testament, but it has received sufficient attention to be considered here as a modern trend of study of the New Testament, regardless of whether it eventually becomes a major trend.[14] Structuralist approaches to literature are intentionally nonhistorical or atemporal.[15] A basic operating assumption

[13] E.g., W. Meeks, "The Stranger from Heaven in Johannine Sectarianism," *Journal of Biblical Literature* 91 (1972): 44–72.

[14] An excellent, compact description and assessment of the structuralist approach is provided by J. Barton, *Reading the Old Testament: Method in Biblical Study* (Philadelphia: Westminster Press, 1984), esp. 104–139; J. W. Rogerson, "Recent Literary Structuralist Approaches to Biblical Interpretation," in *The Churchman* 90 (1976): 165–177. Cf. also D. Patte, *What Is Structural Exegesis?*, Guides to Biblical Scholarship (Philadelphia: Fortress Press, 1976). Especially helpful is M. Lane's introductory essay in the work he edited, *Introduction to Structuralism* (New York: Basic Books, 1970), 11–39.

[15] Cf. Lane, "Introduction," 17: "For the structuralist time as a dimension is no less, but also no more important than any other that might be used in analysis. History is seen as the specific mode of development of a particular system, whose present, or synchronic nature must be fully known before any account can be given of its evolution, or diachronic nature. Moreover, the synchronic structure is seen as being constituted or determined not by any historical process,

is that a text qua text, once it has been produced, creates a life of its own and in this sense becomes detached from the historical situation from which it was produced. Moreover, the student approaches the text not to discover the historical or social realities behind the text to which the text bears witness but, rather, assumes a fundamental correlation between the expressions in the text and the mental structures, broadly conceived, that produced them— hence the quest for deep structures in a text to which the surface structures point or serve as clues. There is, of course, the more general assumption that human thought throughout time has exhibited common, underlying structures that ordinarily exist in pairs, or binary structures. Thus the study of a text is in a sense a hermeneutical task that can put us in touch with the whole range of human knowledge and experience, conceived in the broadest possible sense. Accordingly, structuralist interpretation tends to be conspicuously interdisciplinary.

Here again, structuralist approaches to the New Testament will not be fruitful for congregational studies in the same sense that historical, sociological, and literary approaches are. Even if the New Testament text speaks directly of a historical entity, such as the church at Corinth, structuralist criticism is expressly not interested in either the historical or the social reality of which the text speaks. Even though structuralist criticism shares with literary criticism many of the same concerns, it operates from a different philosophical base. Rather than enabling us to explore the relationship between the historical and the social reality and the form of the narrative to which it bears witness, a structuralist approach helps us generalize about the deep structures found in a New Testament text and compare them with the deep structures reflected in the story that a congregation tells. Even so, because of the ahistorical methodological approach of structuralism, it is difficult to relate the study of the text to the congregation as an empirical reality, in either its ancient or its modern form. At best, this sort of study clarifies the congregation as an idea or a concept, but even that is limited.

4. *Canonical criticism.* In one sense, canonical criticism demonstrates the aforementioned observation that biblical criticism has paid increasing attention to the role of the church in producing and preserving the canon.[16] Here, of course, church is understood in the general sense, but even so, canonical criticism recognizes the importance of specific communities of faith in formulating the biblical witness. Like redaction criticism, canonical criticism tends to emphasize the final form of the biblical text. But unlike redaction criticism, it is less interested in the author as a theologian than in the church as a creator and shaper of the biblical witness.

---

but by the network of existing structural relations. Hence structuralism is rather atemporal than strictly ahistorical."

[16] Cf. J. A. Sanders, *Canon and Community: A Guide to Canonical Criticism,* Guides to Biblical Scholarship (Philadelphia: Fortress Press, 1984). For its application to the New Testament, cf. B. Childs, *The New Testament As Canon: An Introduction* (Philadelphia: Fortress Press, 1984).

Because canonical criticism operates with a more general notion of church than does form criticism, or even redaction criticism, its impact on congregational studies is proportionately less direct. To be sure, canonical critics appreciate the degree to which the church has participated in the canonical process, not only as a recipient or even a transmitter, but also as an active shaper of the biblical materials. Accordingly, they insist that a biblical text be understood both as a message addressed to and read or heard by religious communities and as a message that reflects the earlier conversation or dialogue in which ancient religious communities were involved. Thus, for example, 1 and 2 Chronicles should not be read as a text addressed to a reader, ancient or modern, but as a text in which the chronicler, and the communities he represents, is actively interpreting and appropriating earlier traditions in light of new situations. The canonical shape of the biblical writings, then, reveals not several separate "books" whose message the interpreter is trying to discern but an "internal conversation" within the biblical writings that the interpreter can both hear and join.

The degree to which canonical criticism gains a specific understanding of these religious communities, and gives concrete shape to them, will determine its relevance to congregational studies.

New Testament studies over the last two centuries have, if anything, demonstrated a consistent interest in the congregation, as both a concept and an empirical reality. Indeed, as New Testament scholarship has pursued the agenda of historical criticism, it has developed hypotheses concerning ancient Christian congregations as a way of explaining certain features of the text as well as accounting for the history of various traditions. This concern for concrete communities of faith has grown with the rising interest in the social history of early Christianity, and there is every reason to believe that this interst will continue. The direct relevance of other trends in New Testament scholarship—notably the study of the New Testament as literature, structuralist criticism, and canonical criticism—is less easily discerned, even though each provides an approach that can both benefit the study of modern congregations and be benefited by such study.

Teaching the New Testament with a Congregational Focus

In a seminary curriculum, students ordinarily study the New Testament through (1) courses of general introduction to the New Testament; (2) courses in particular New Testament writings, usually exegesis courses; and (3) topical courses treating various aspects of New Testament theology. Probably none of these is currently taught as if the congregation were the object toward whose well-being the curriculum is primarily directed, much less as if congregation as a paradigm were providing the organizing structures. We might speculate what the first two would look like were this the case.

1. *New Testament Introduction.* Interestingly, the history of New Testament Introduction as a discipline, as reflected in the textbooks for this

subject, may be said to have shifted already toward the congregation. The most recent comprehensive work in this genre, H. Koester's two-volume *History and Literature of Early Christianity* is distinguished from its predecessors precisely by its stated purpose "to present the history of early Christian churches."[17] With its explicit historical orientation, the work belongs to a tradition begun by F. C. Baur. The decision to divide the terrain geographically and to treat the development of early Christianity in the various sections of the Roman Empire owes much to W. Bauer.[18] The effort to relate the writings of the New Testament to all other early Christian writings and to introduce the writings of the New Testament to the world of late antiquity, broadly conceived, reflects the legacy of R. Bultmann, to whom the work is dedicated.[19] This introduction represents the drive toward historical concreteness that began in the nineteenth century. The student who is introduced to the New Testament through this work thus will acquire a much greater awareness of early Christian communities, the complex religious traditions present in those communities, and the process through which these various traditions—often competing with one another—finally became crystallized in the writings of the New Testament. The student will also learn about the many other noncanonical writings and will become acquainted with the canonical process through which orthodox and heterodox positions were fought out.

The importance of this shift should be underscored. In the more traditional New Testament introduction, the student is introduced to the writings of the New Testament with very little if any attention to the noncanonical writings and with equally little attention to early Christian communities as the crucibles of early Christianity. Whether the use of H. Koester's *Introduction* as a textbook would enable seminarians to appreciate the congregation as the purpose toward which their training is directed depends, of course, on how it is taught. But at least Koester's work represents a move in this direction.[20]

---

[17] H. Koester, *Introduction to the New Testament: Volume One: History, Culture, and Religion of the Hellenistic Age*, Hermeneia Foundations and Facets (Philadelphia: Fortress Press, 1982), xxi. Cf. reviews by A. J. Malherbe and G. Luedemann, *Religious Studies Review* 10 (1984): 112–120.

[18] W. Bauer, *Orthodoxy and Heresy in Earliest Christianity* (Philadelphia: Fortress Press, 1971).

[19] Koester, *Introduction*, xxiii.

[20] Another approach to introducing the New Testament, in this case to undergraduates, is provided by W. Meeks, "Imagining the Early Christians: Some Problems in an Introductory Course in the New Testament," *Perspectives in Religious Studies* 2 (1975): 3–12. Interestingly enough, his way into the material is "congregational" in that he begins by reconstructing three actual ancient religious communities—Jewish, pagan, and Christian—at Dura Europos, using archaeological materials combined with historical and literary sources. By getting the students to imagine actual living communities of faith, he poses the various historical and methodological problems that the course will pursue, and then he finally introduces the literary sources to be studied, mainly the New Testament writings, but also noncanonical Christian writings and other sources from the period.

2. *Exegesis courses.* The choice of material will obviously dictate the suitability of orienting certain New Testament writings toward a congregational paradigm. As we have already noted, although the Gospels can be linked to identifiable streams of early Christianity, and in some cases to identifiable communities or groups of communities, the degree to which they address the needs of particular congregations still is not clear.

The case is quite different, however, with the epistolary material. All seven of the authentic Pauline letters are addressed to named congregations; at least four other New Testament letters are addressed to what appear to be local congregations; and the Book of Revelation is addressed to a group of seven churches in Asia Minor. In these cases, the hermeneutical move is quite different, as modern congregations serve as the closest analogue to the original recipients of these writings.

Even within the epistolary material, however, the range of possibilities is limited. One of the most intriguing possibilities for pedagogical experimentation would be to develop a course on the church at Corinth, not so much as an exegetical study of the text of 1 and 2 Corinthians, but as a case study from antiquity suitable for ministers in a curriculum oriented toward the welfare of the congregation. Indeed, as the various sociological studies of the Corinthian church have pointed out, there is an abundance of source material for such a course.[21] These sources include both the two letters that Paul wrote to the Corinthians and his letters probably written to other churches from Corinth. There is also the account of the church's beginning in Acts 18 as well as the letter of 1 Clement, which was addressed to the church at Corinth near the end of the first century. In addition to the canonical material, there is much source material pertaining to the city of Corinth, which was collected by J. Murphy-O'Connor.[22]

Besides the abundance of sources, there are several recent, well-conceived studies on Corinth and Pauline Christianity, drawing on the social sciences.[23] These have already begun to move beyond the traditional commentaries by analyzing some of the problems in the Corinthian church in terms of their social dynamics, and these analyses have in turn begun to be correlated with theological issues. This makes it possible to examine Paul's theological method from other perspectives than his appropriation of Old Testament traditions and early Christian traditions. Indeed, it allows ample opportunity to examine the theological method as it is formulated and implemented between the minister and the congregation. These resources also orient the study of the New Testament text toward the congregation itself as the object of study.

[21] Cf. Gager, *Kingdom and Community;* Theissen, *Social Setting;* Meeks, *The First Urban Christians;* Malherbe, *Social Aspects.*

[22] J. Murphy-O'Connor, *St. Paul's Corinth: Texts and Archaeology,* Good News Studies, vol. 6 (Wilmington, Del.: Michael Glazier, 1983).

[23] Esp. Theissen, Meeks, and Malherbe.

As already mentioned, how the case study is related to the modern congregation requires a different pedagogical move, largely based on analogy. But it does offer an opportunity to address such questions as the degree to which early Christian practice—as opposed to statements from the canonical text—should provide norms for modern Christian practice. It also offers another angle on the perennial problem of distance and proximity, perhaps allowing the students to see the historical and cultural distance even more vividly, while at the same time recognizing the many instances of existential proximity.

If one chooses to structure in this way a course—indeed an entire seminary curriculum—the inevitable charge already brought against historical criticism will be that the student is being introduced to something besides the text. After all, the call for reform being issued by literary critics, structuralist critics, and canonical critics is that the study of the text itself has been replaced by the study of something beyond the text, either the history that is reconstructed from the text or the social, empirical reality to which it attests. This criticism will be especially trenchant if it stems from a Barthian insistence on the Word as a mediating agent.

Summary and Conclusion

This paper has argued that the current New Testament scholarship favors the study of the congregation, even though this has not been its motivating force. The impetus generated by historical criticism has created a drive for historical concreteness that, at crucial stages in New Testament scholarhsip, has broadened our understanding of the early Christian communities. Much of the current research in New Testament scholarship pertains both directly and indirectly to the study of the congregation as both concept and empirical reality. As the study of modern congregations continues and refines its methods, its results will help illuminate the New Testament material, both the writings themselves and our historical understanding of early Christianity.

To be sure, major trends of current New Testament scholarhsip are under way whose direct impact on congregational studies is not obvious, although some possible points of contact have been noted and suggested. Were the congregation to become a more focal concern of seminary curricula, it would be interesting to see whether it could provide an organizing paradigm around which the several methods of biblical criticism might meet. It might be possible to conceive a course in which the congregation, say Corinth, is the subject matter and in which the several texts pertaining to this church are examined from each of the several disciplines of historical, literary, structuralist, and canonical criticism, with a view to determining the ways in which each broadens our empirical understanding of the congregation at Corinth.

THE HISTORIAN AND THE CONGREGATION

E. Brooks Holifield

Most American churches and synagogues have proclaimed, in one form or another, a universal message. They have viewed themselves as a part of worldwide communities and ancient traditions, and they have often seen their task as the propagation of their faith throughout the world. Yet one of the ironies of American religious history has been the tension between the affirmation of such universal aims and the persistence of an intense localism that has shaped the religious perceptions and behavior of most Americans with religious commitments.

The locus that has formed the religious life of most believers is the congregation, a tenacious sociological reality with its own internal symbols and patterns of interactions. The congregation has been the primary social group within which religious commitments in America have found expression. Yet no one has tried to tell the story of religion in America from a perspective formed by the analysis of the congregation, and the oversight is odd, for that tenacious localism and the manifold challenges to it deserve some attention.

This essay has a modest purpose. Of necessity it must be merely suggestive, for we have no accumulated body of historical research on congregations and their typical activities. Yet even the tentative historical typology that I shall propose raises some questions about the conventional perspective on a number of standard topics—and commonplace assertions— in American religious history. And I believe that one can sustain the claim that the activities of congregations have exhibited a discernible shape or pattern, or more precisely, a changing series of shapes, during the past three hundred years, even though I cannot promise to sustain that claim in this brief paper.

I should like to take a three-hundred-year slice of American history, from roughly 1607 to 1907, and suggest that one can find patterns that cut across standard denominational distinctions and offer an altered vision of religion in America. In referring to "magisterial" congregations, to the congregation as "sanctuary," and to "congenial" congregations, I do not assume that these three types exhaust the range of religious options. But they suggest a point of view that can usefully supplement—and sometimes correct—conclusions derived from other methods of interpreting the history of religion in America. A study of congregations can alter our understanding of the history and modify our conception of what we are doing when we teach it.

Magisterial Congregations

The dominant category in the interpretation of American religious history has customarily been the *denomination,* and it has been tempting for historians to read back into the early seventeenth century the denominational identity and stability that marked later periods. Such a procedure has a certain plausibility and usefulness, for the early colonial congregations did coalesce into identifiable groupings defined, in part, by their adherence to distinguishable traditions. Those traditions—Catholic, Reformed, Lutheran, Anglican—preceded the colonial congregations and helped determine their structures and activities. But the congregations preceded the unified and stable organizations that we have come to call denominations. Hence to understand the movement from European traditions to American denominations, one must look closely at the shape and function of the local congregations.

By 1650 American colonists had created at least 112 religious congregations, which served not only as gatherings for worship but also as centers of social authority. Historians have regularly observed the relative fragility in the southern colonies of congregations that had to serve an area extending from sixty to over one hundred miles in length. But they have not noticed as frequently that even on the southern frontier the formation of churches regularly preceded the establishment of new counties and county courts, so that congregational gatherings became the customary occasions for reading official proclamations, conducting elections, posting provincial laws, and circulating grievance petitions.[1] The southern congregations were magisterial in a double sense; they served as gatherings for the propagation of authoritative religious and moral instruction, and they performed official functions of the civil magistracy.

The magisterial character of congregations in New England was even more pronounced. Church membership conferred rights of citizenship, and in Massachusetts and New Haven the law admitted only the inner core of the congregation—the full members—to the status of freemen. No town in Massachusetts Bay could exist as a corporate body in the absence of a congregation. The organizing of a church therefore brought a fledgling community one step closer to recognition as an independent order under its own local governance. It was symbolic of the congregation's status that the

---

[1] George Maclaren Brydon, *Virginia's Mother Church and the Political Conditions Under Which It Grew,* vol. 1 (Richmond: Virginia Historical Society, 1947), 181; Patricia U. Bonomi and Peter R. Eisenstadt, "Church Adherence in the Eighteenth-Century British American Colonies," *William and Mary Quarterly* 39 (April 1982): 263.

meetinghouse in which the Bay colonists worshiped served also as the court house and legislative hall in which they governed their communities. And it was equally symbolic that they sometimes named "center committees" to ensure that the meetinghouse be located, as precisely as possible, in the geographical center of the town.[2]

The symbolic rituals associated with the formation and the activities of religious congregations intensified the aura of magisterial authority that they conveyed. In Massachusetts Bay, the gathering of a church was a public event at which the governor of the colony was always expected. In Virginia, magistrates not only passed legislation requiring church attendance but also used ecclesiastical ritual to confirm their own authority. The governor, Lord Delaware, attended the services of the earliest Virginia congregation attended by councilors, captains, officers, and gentlemen, with a guard of fifty soldiers dressed in red cloaks.[3] The congregations' reliance on the trappings of the state may have reflected their weakness and instability, but more probably the ritual and legal alliances between congregations and magistrates simply displayed the traditional assumption that churches were entitled to a status of privilege and authority.[4]

Throughout the colonies, in any case, congregations assumed responsibility for public order, and in New England especially, disciplinary hearings became one of the most common functions of congregational meetings. Congregations admonished their members for offenses ranging from intemperance and illicit sex to defamation and excessive profits. The colonists carefully distinguished congregational from civil admonitions, but that in no way diminished the sense of authority that congregations assumed over their members.[5] Even colonial Jewish congregations, which lacked the Protestant sense of alliance with forces of public order, tried to emulate the coercive, semiautonomous medieval synagogue by purchasing cemetery land, monopolizing education, supervising the preparation of food, and engaging in other activities that ensured congregational authority over all significant public Jewish behavior.[6]

The authority of colonial congregations has often been viewed simply as a reflection of clerical authority. A closer look at the congregations, though, reveals the surprising extent to which the maintenance of religion—and of its magisterial authority—resulted from lay initiative. Throughout the middle

[2] See Ola Winslow, *Meetinghouse Hill 1630–1783* (New York: Macmillan, 1952), 30, 51; David Hall, *The Faithful Shepherd* (Chapel Hill: University of North Carolina Press, 1972), 150.

[3] Winslow, *Meetinghouse Hill*, 32; Brydon, *Virginia's Mother Church*, vol. 1, 16; R. H. Potter, *Hartford's First Church* (Hartford: First Church, 1932), 91.

[4] Timothy L. Smith, "Congregation, State, and Denomination: The Forming of the American Religious Structure," *William and Mary Quarterly* 25 (1968): 155–176.

[5] Emil Oberholzer, *Delinquent Saints* (New York: Columbia University Press, 1956).

[6] Jack Wertheimer, "The American Synagogue Historically Considered," paper presented at the annual meeting of the American Society of Church History, December 28, 1984.

and southern colonies, congregations gathered for worship even before ministers became available to serve them, and lay vestries replaced Anglican bishops as the parishes' overseers. Trinity Church in New York City began, for instance, at the instigation of twelve laypersons who organized themselves as "managers of the Church of England," purchased land, elected a rector (who traveled to England for ordination), and constituted themselves as a vestry to administer the affairs of the congregation. Such actions were typical of colonial congregations outside New England. From Pennsylvania to Georgia, dozens of congregations organized themselves without a minister and then issued pleas for clerical leadership.[7]

Even in New England, where the clergy were especially prominent, the official theory declared that churches were to be formed through covenants of the laity—and only then to elect their ministers. The clerical theologians directed the procedures, to be sure, but the argument that New England Puritanism was a clerical imposition overlooks the importance of lay initiative both in the formation of churches and in the creation of the religious ethos. A closer look at the congregation would shift the angle of vision on colonial religion by revealing the extent of lay initiative and authority.[8]

The assertiveness of the laity in the congregations became increasingly troublesome to colonial ministers. The Anglican commissary in Virginia, James Blair, complained that colonial churches treated ministers as mere "hirelings," and Gottlieb Mittelberger in Pennsylvania lamented the tendency of congregations there to hire ministers by the year, "like cowherds in Germany." And the laity even of New England congregations refused to act in the way that the theologians had expected. The Boston congregation supported the recalcitrant Anne Hutchinson; the Salem congregation followed the eccentric Roger Williams; and the primary opposition to the "halfway covenant" came from pietistic laity who disliked the thought of any innovations in church admission procedures.[9]

The second generation of New England ministers encountered resistance from congregations whom they failed to please. The first generation usually stayed with one congregation for their entire ministry, but most of the second tried at least two different churches. As younger men took over the pulpits, the congregations insisted on contracts, often with restrictions on automatic tenure. By the 1650s, local churches were imposing a "con-

---

[7] Bonomi and Eisenstadt, "Church Adherence," 248; Smith, "Congregation, State, and Denomination," 161–173; Clifford P. Morehouse, *Trinity: Mother of Churches* (New York: Seabury Press, 1973), 10.

[8] Winslow, *Meetinghouse Hill*, 20–25; David Hall, "Toward a History of Popular Religion in Early New England," *William and Mary Quarterly* 41 (1984): 49–55; Baird Tipson, "Judge Thy Practice by This Pattern," paper presented at the annual meeting of the American Society of Church History, December 29, 1984.

[9] Bonomi and Eisenstadt, "Church Adherence," 247; Robert G. Pope, *The Half-Way Covenant: Church Membership in Puritan New England* (Princeton, N.J.: Princeton University Press, 1969); Hall, *The Faithful Shepherd*, 93–120, 156–196; Philip F. Gura, *A Glimpse of Sion's Glory* (Middletown, Conn.: Wesleyan University Press, 1984), 31–92.

tractual" understanding of ministry throughout the New England colonies. By the early eighteenth century, ordination sermons regularly warned young ministers about the "stiff and turbulent spirits" they would meet in their churches, and during the conflicts over revivalism during the 1740s, stubborn congregations dismissed dozens of ministers with whom they disagreed. Indeed, during that "Great Awakening" more than one hundred groups of laypersons separated from their old congregations, usually in defiance of their ministers, and formed new ones, and dozens of additional groups withdrew temporarily. No adequate history of American religion can overlook the tradition of lay restiveness that began in the colonial era—and the initial locus of that restiveness was the congregation.[10]

This unrest should not be confused with indifference. A close look at local congregations casts doubt on the traditional depiction of colonial religious history as a story of initial fervor, subsequent decline, revivalist renewal, and ensuing indifference, broken only by further revivalism. According to that depiction, eighteenth-century Americans remained, despite the Awakening, resistant to clerical exhortations. The typical assertion has been that by 1789 only 5 to 10 percent of colonial Americans belonged to local churches. But once again, the close study of local congregations fails to support the traditional assessment. Edwin Gaustad's *Historical Atlas of Religion in America* presents the patterns of congregational growth in eight colonial denominations. By 1700, he found, 369 congregations had been formed throughout the colonies; in 1740, the number had risen to 1,176; and by 1780, there were 2,731.[11]

From 1700 to 1780, in other words, the number of local congregations in eight of the largest American religious groups increased more than sixfold. During a period when the white population increased by 888 percent, the number of congregations rose at least 640 percent. Using those numbers along with others, Patricia Bonomi and Peter Eisenstadt concluded that although the percentage of church adherents within the total population did decline during the eighteenth century, the percentage that attended local congregations ranged from 80 percent in 1700 to 59 percent in 1780. The criteria for full membership varied from church to church, and the number of full members was surely smaller than the number of persons who attended regularly. But the increase in the number of congregations, and the sizable number of persons who attended their services, provide indices of religious behavior that are more useful to the historian than are estimates of the number of full members.[12]

The congregations flourished and encouraged a broad variety of religious

[10] Winslow, *Meetinghouse Hill*, 211–228; Hall, *The Faithful Shepherd*, 176–178; C. C. Goen, *Revivalism and Separatism in New England, 1740–1800* (New Haven, Conn.: Yale University Press, 1962), 327.

[11] Bonomi and Eisenstadt, "Church Adherence," 245–286; Edwin S. Gaustad, *Historical Atlas of Religion in America* (New York: Harper & Row, 1962), 3–5.

[12] Bonomi and Eisenstadt, "Church Adherence," 245–286.

activities. Colonial theologians wrote primarily for and within congregations; Samuel Willard developed his massive *Compleat Body of Divinity* (1726) as a series of lectures to a congregation, and most other theologians worked in a similar manner. Colonial ministers learned the arts of their profession under the tutelage of older preachers who were serving congregations. A considerable body of colonial music developed in religious congregations. Much of the language of colonial political discourse—language about covenants, compacts, duties, and rights—received its initial articulation in the congregations. And the American denominations resulted from the cumulative influence of both European traditions and congregational histories.

The Congregation As Sanctuary

In the decades following the Revolution, the religious congregation lost some of its magisterial authority and scope. This change reflected, in part, an economic transition from a self-subsistence agricultural economy, organized around household industries, to a nascent industrial economy built around the factory. The economic changes produced two contrasting social patterns: the multiplication of towns and the expansion of the agricultural frontier (and hence of slavery). That leap from the family-craft system to mercantile and factory capitalism also helped produce an increasingly segmented society. It produced firmer boundaries between the domestic and the economic, as workers began to live in one place and work in another. It established sharper divisions between men and women, as the new organization of trades, crafts, and factories left urban women at home in domestic rather than public roles. It deepened the chasm between slave and free by opening new markets for southern cotton and rice. It intensified the gap between the public and the private, as the household became not the locus of production but a retreat from the marketplace. It drove a wedge between capital and labor, as capitalists tried to increase productivity and workers formed "unions of the trades" to protect themselves. It established new lines of division between town and country, for the new commerce required urban concentration, produced urban wealth, and exalted urban values.[13] And it produced a host of new institutions and voluntary organizations that gradually assumed functions that once had belonged solely to the congregations.

The social changes coincided with the Second Great Awakening, a sustained revival that gradually altered the shape of American religion. The alteration was registered initially by the multiplication of new congregations. Rather than linger on the outskirts of the frontier camp meeting, marveling at the excesses of religious ecstasy, the historian would do well to follow the advice of Donald Mathews and see the awakening as an "organizing movement" of unprecedented scale in America. The aim of the evangelists was to

[13] See E. Brooks Holifield, *A History of Pastoral Care in America* (Nashville: Abingdon Press, 1983), 113–114.

organize religious congregations, and they were stunningly successful. In 1780 there were fewer than 3,000 American congregations; by 1820 there were at least 10,904. A survey conducted by the Bureau of the Census in 1906 revealed that 3,637 existing congregations traced their beginnings to the period before 1800 but that 21,929 claimed to have been founded between 1800 and 1849. The figures are ambiguous, but they exhibit the coincidence of the Second Awakening and an unprecedented enthusiasm for organizing new congregations.[14]

The awakening, the new economic order, and the debate over slavery helped alter the tone of the congregations' religious activities. The revival spawned an array of Bible classes, Sunday Schools, mission societies, devotional gatherings, and prayer meetings that brought increasing numbers of people together in small groups. The "new devotionalism" signified, on one level, a retreat from the divisive and violent struggle over slavery. But among Protestants it also embodied the piety of the revival. Among Catholics it reflected the emergence under Pius IX of a renewed accent on the sacrament of penance, indulgence prayers, sacred heart devotionals, parish missions, and devotion to the saints. Among Jews the new devotionalism appeared at mid-century when immigrants created a variety of fraternal societies, charities, clinics, and clubs and defined the synagogue more narrowly as a house of prayer and education.[15]

This transition did not by any means signal an onset of religious indifference to social issues. It signified, rather, a shift in the way that religious men and women organized themselves to oppose social evils. Ralph Waldo Emerson noted the change in 1844: "The Church, or religious party," he said, "is falling from the Church nominal, and is appearing in temperance and non-resistance societies; in movements of abolitionists and of socialists . . . composed of . . . all the soul of the soldiery of dissent."[16] Reformers created new agencies—the benevolent empire of voluntary societies—to wage their crusades against social evils, and the societies gradually assumed the public tasks that the colonial congregations had undertaken. Local con-

[14] Gaustad, *Historical Atlas*, 43; Donald Mathews, "The Second Great Awakening As an Organizing Process, 1780–1830," *American Quarterly* 21 (1969): 23–43; *Bureau of the Census Special Reports—Religious Bodies: 1906*, 99.

[15] Donald Scott, *From Office to Profession: The New England Ministry 1750–1850* (Philadelphia: University of Pennsylvania Press, 1978); Sidney E. Mead, "The Rise of the Evangelical Conception of the Ministry," in *Ministry in Historical Perspectives*, ed. H. R. Niebuhr and D. D. Williams (New York: Harper & Row, 1956), 229; Jay P. Dolan, *The Immigrant Church: New York's Irish and German Catholics 1815–1865* (Baltimore: Johns Hopkins University Press, 1975); Jay P. Dolan, *Catholic Revivalism: The American Experience* (Notre Dame, Ind.: University of Notre Dame Press, 1978); Wertheimer, "American Synagogue"; Ann Taves, "Publishing, Literacy, and the Romanization of Catholic Devotional Practices in the United States, 1840–1880," paper delivered at the annual meeting of the American Society of Church History, December 27, 1984.

[16] Ralph Waldo Emerson, "New England Reformers," *Essays: Second Series, Emerson's Complete Works*, Riverside ed., vol. 3 (London: George Routledge and Sons, 1883), 239.

gregations sometimes supported the voluntary societies from afar, but increasingly the white congregations, at least, became enclaves of inwardness.

Congregations may have abandoned some of their earlier magisterial functions in the political order, but they retained their assertive guidance over their own members and even expanded the range of their assertions in new directions. To understand this assertiveness, one must observe the increasingly important distinction between urban and frontier congregations.

The congregations on the rural frontier continued, even intensified, the older ideal of discipline. Frontier religion was only superficially individualistic. Indeed, the frontier congregations became, in William Warren Sweet's phrase, the "moral courts" of the countryside. In Baptist church covenants, Methodist classes, and Presbyterian sessions, Christians pledged themselves to "admonish each other," and so they did, often insisting on a conformity of dress, language, and behavior that bears a marked resemblance to the revolutionary discipline of Maoist China in the twentieth century.[17]

Urban congregations also maintained internal discipline, though to a lesser extent and with more subtlety. Yet they gradually distinguished themselves in style and tone from their rural counterparts. Located alongside new lecture halls, opera houses, libraries, town halls, and lycea, they abandoned many of the social functions that congregations in the countryside still maintained. But they also reflected the tone of their urban surroundings, especially in their preoccupation with the ideal of gentility.[18]

When Frances Trollope toured the United States in 1827, she observed that church gatherings were the occasions when "all display is made, and all fashionable distinction sought." A stranger from Europe would be inclined, she said, to suppose "that the places of worship were the theatres and cafes of the place." Urban congregations increasingly thought of themselves as refined and polished, and they insisted that their ministers adhere to their canons of refinement. The result was an outpouring of handbooks instructing ministers how to be delicate and genteel, the introduction of choirs and new hymnals to maintain musical decorum, careful attention to the etiquette of pew rentals, a tendency for ministers to preach in silk gloves and formal attire, and the remarkable spread of "chaste, elegant, and commodious" buildings in Gothic and Grecian styles.[19] An awareness of that preoccupation

[17] T. Scott Miyakawa, *Protestants and Pioneers: Individualism and Conformity on the American Frontier* (Chicago: University of Chicago Press, 1964); see, for example, Garland A. Hendricks, *Biography of a Country Church* (Nashville: Broadman Press, 1950), 18.

[18] Scott, *From Office to Profession*, 151.

[19] Frances M. Trollope, *Domestic Manners of the Americans* (New York: Dodd, Mead, & Co., 1901; 1st ed., 1831), 102; Holifield, *History of Pastoral Care in America*, 111–144; Floyd S. Bennett, *Methodist Church on Shockoe Hill* (Richmond: Centenary Methodist Church, 1962), 36.

with gentility and decorum casts new light on familiar religious movements: It was the interest in congregational decorum, for instance, rather than the importation of European ideas, that prompted the emergence of Reform Judaism in the United States.[20] And it was the assertive style of urban Catholic congregations, as well as ethnic tensions, that led to the trusteeism controversy that threatened to divide the Catholic church in America.

The local congregations retained some of their older functions. Though Protestants began to build seminaries to train ministers, the schools stayed in close touch with local congregations, and theologians still wrote largely about the issues that mattered to the men and women in the pews. Some of the leading theologians of the period—for example, Horace Bushnell—spent their entire careers as ministers of local churches.

The new congregational "sanctuary," marked by the new devotionalism, represented a certain disengagement from the wider society. Yet part of the irony of the change was the way in which it provided enclaves of autonomy within which black slaves, free blacks, and urban women could develop leadership and authority. Throughout the nineteenth century, women out-numbered men in the congregations by about two to one. The men main-tained their traditional authority in the institution, but as the new pastoral handbooks suggest, they became increasingly sensitive to the approval of women members. And women found in the congregations a chance to organize themselves, initially in local missionary societies but eventually in wider networks of organization for missions and benevolent causes. Anne Firor Scott was surely correct when she designated the congregation as a crucial stepping-stone in the progress of women from the pedestal to pol-itics.[21]

In even more dramatic fashion, the congregation served as one sphere in the antebellum period in which blacks could assume leadership in a public organization. The black congregations were often quite similar to the white ones: They cultivated the same piety of inwardness; in the cities they often idealized gentility; they pledged to exercise the same kind of "watchfulness" over each member; and they had the same interest in foreign missions. But they also retained the variety of public functions and reforming instincts that most white congregations had abandoned. They served as social centers, reform societies, and, where possible, political forums. It was no surprise that the leadership of the black community in the nineteenth century emerged almost exclusively from the black congregations. Moreover, that

[20] Leon A. Jick, *The Americanization of the Synagogue, 1820–1870* (Hanover, N.H.: Brandeis University Press, 1976).

[21] Joseph Kett, *Rites of Passage* (New York: Basic Books, 1977), 65; Anne Firor Scott, *The Southern Lady* (Chicago: University of Chicago Press, 1970); Joan R. Gundersen, "The Local Parish As a Female Institution: The Experience of All Saints Episcopal Church in Frontier Minnesota," *Church History* 55 (1986); 307–322.

pattern of social involvement served as a guide for the organizers of "institutional churches" in the American cities after the Civil War.[22]

The mainline congregational "sanctuary" was, on the whole, a conservative force in the society, but it could unwittingly subvert the traditional
values that its leaders espoused. Despite its implicit and explicit ideology of
black and feminine subordination, the congregation as sanctuary could serve,
even if unintentionally, as an agency of empowerment for the powerless. It is
the study of the congregation that might best illumine that ironic paradox of
conservatism and subversion in American religious history.

Congenial Congregations

The Civil War, the postwar industrial economy, and the influx of new
immigrants led to new styles of congregational life. The carnage of war, the
emergence of new technologies, and prominence of industrial barons, the
conflicts between capital and labor, the philosophical and scientific interests
in natural vitalities, and the interest in sports and the cult of virility in the
popular culture all created a sense of unease with the sentimentality of the
antebellum era and a sensitivity to images of power and vitality. The postwar
cultural ethos helped engender a new image of the congregation. Older
images remained and thousands of congregations shaped themselves in
accordance with them. But some postwar congregations, especially in the
cities, began to assume a new shape and style.

In 1860 there were about 51,000 American congregations; by 1906 there
were 212,230. Most of them appeared in the small towns and countryside,
and many of those proved tenacious in their adherence to older images of
congregational life. But among the 17,906 congregations in the 160 cities
with a population larger than 25,000—and among many other congregations
in smaller cities—there was an eagerness to develop new patterns.[23]

Between 1870 and 1900, parish life in many urban congregations under-
went what one observer at the time called a "complete revolution." The
symbol of change seemed to him to be the "church parlor." Growing numbers of congregations transformed themselves into centers that not only were
open for worship but also were available for Sunday school concerts, church
socials, women's meetings, youth groups, girls' guilds, boys' brigades, singing classes, and a host of other organizations and activities.[24]

These new convivial congregations became centers for performance,
whether by popular princes of the pulpit, new trained and vested choirs, or,

[22] Albert J. Raboteau, *Slave Religion* (New York: Oxford University Press, 1977), 65–75, 163,
179, 204; James M. Simms, *The First Colored Baptist Church in North America* (New York:
Negro Universities Press, 1969; 1st ed., 1888), 57–59, 225.

[23] Gaustad, *Historical Atlas*, 43–44; *Bureau of the Census, Special Reports*, 21, 69.

[24] G. B. Willcox, *The Pastor Amidst His Flock* (New York: American Tract Society, 1890), 107.

occasionally, orchestras performing during worship services. They also became centers for social fellowship. Henry Ward Beecher in 1872 urged congregations to "multiply picnics," and many quickly proceeded beyond picnics to gymnasiums, parish houses, camps, baseball teams, and military drill groups, with one church report in 1897 asserting that "uniforms, guns and equipment are as essential as the Bible and the Hymnal in the advance of the work." In addition to all that, they multiplied traditional groups: women's missionary societies, church school societies, and altar guilds.[25]

The new-style congregations proclaimed an ideology of "friendliness, democracy, and solidarity." They encouraged new forms of shared participation. During the late 1860s, many churches that had raised their budgets through pew rentals and subscriptions began instead to have weekly offerings and to adopt the "envelope system" for fund raising. Preachers like Phillip Brooks made it a point to preach to their congregations "as a man might speak to his friend." Members were encouraged to give memorial windows, tablets, altars, and fonts in honor of their loved ones, with the symbolic effect that the churches visually honored their own revered members.[26]

Some of the new activism represented an effort to attract men into the churches. The women still outnumbered them; in 1906 about 61 percent of Protestants and 51 percent of Catholics were women. Some of the preachers believed that only "parish organization" could attract men; others, especially Protestants, began to preach about "muscular Christianity" and to depict Jesus as a brave and valorous hero who challenged money changers and faced down hostile mobs. The study of the congregation might reveal the extent to which the liberal social gospel tried to recruit men; Washington Gladden, for one, preached his social gospel sermons on Sunday nights in services designed especially for business and professional men. It might also reveal, however, the extent to which women in local congregations, especially black congregations, expanded their own traditions of social ministry.[27]

In evaluating the effectiveness of the social gospel, moreover, the historian might look not simply at the influence of the theologians but at the daily activities of the "institutional churches" as well. By 1906 New York City alone was said to have 112 such churches, Chicago about 25, and every other major city at least 1; large black congregations embodied the "institutional" ideal throughout the South. In accord with that ideal, congregations extended their activities to meet the social needs of their neighborhoods and regions. St. Bartholomew's in New York offered ethnic missions, an industrial

[25] Henry Ward Beecher, *Yale Lectures in Preaching* (New York: Fords, Howard, and Hulbert, 1892), 155, 159; Ihna T. T. Frary, ed., *Village Green to City Center 1843–1943: Centennial of the Euclid Avenue Congregational Church* (Cleveland: Euclid Avenue Church, 1943), 141.

[26] Jeffrey Brackett, ed., *Trinity Church in the City of Boston* (Boston: Trinity Church, 1933). I made these generalizations on the basis of my reading of thirteen congregational histories.

[27] Holifield, *History of Pastoral Care*, 170–171; Cheryl Townsend Gilkes, "'Together and in Harness': Women's Traditions in the Sanctified Church," *Signs* 10 (1985): 678–699.

school, kindergartens, an employment bureau, a clinic with fifty physicians, a legal service that handled four thousand cases yearly, a workers' club, a girls' boarding house, a circulating library, a gymnasium, and dozens of clubs and classes for the tenement dwellers of the surrounding neighborhoods. Catholic congregations made similar investments of energy in their parochial schools. And it was no accident that the Jewish Reconstructionist Movement—a movement to redefine the congregation as a social center embodying the fruits of a Jewish civilization—first took institutional form during this period. [28]

By the end of the century, though, the congregations were beginning to show some of the strains that were to burden them in later decades. The independent evangelists, like Dwight L. Moody, created a supracongregational institution, mass revivalism, that could make the routine of congregational acitivity seem stodgy. The universities provided the new setting for the theologians and biblical critics, whose interests gradually shifted from the problems of congregations to the issues of academic guilds. And the formation of the Federal Council of Churches in 1908 symbolized the emergence of a new style of religious bureaucracy that eventually shifted the initiative from the local congregations to national and denominational officials.

So What?

The development of religious congregations in America has been much more complicated than my rough historical typology suggests. Yet even this simple narrative suggests that an examination of the congregation can shift our perspective on many familiar topics, from the effects of the Second Awakening to the changing social location of theology. An accent on the congregation also alters the task of teaching religious history in the classroom. For many of us, the aim of historical teaching has been to help students acquire a greater measure of self-understanding by helping them identify the traditions and movements that have shaped them, or to encounter traditions that challenge their conventional views of themselves. Our aims have paralleled the intentions of existential theologians who see their task as the clarifying and transforming of self-understanding. We have been preoccupied with the topic of identity, thereby reflecting our own indebtedness to the psychological categories of a therapeutic culture.

Such a preoccupation has not been without benefits, however, and I do not recommend abandoning it. But especially in the theological seminary, the historical curriculum can also serve other purposes, including helping ministers better understand the social institution in which they labor. The historical study of the congregation can uncover images that still retain their

---

[28] Ferenc Morton Szasz, *The Divided Mind of Protestant America, 1880–1930* (Tuscaloosa: University of Alabama Press, 1982), 48–55.

power in the local churches. Indeed, almost every church will have members who vaguely believe that the congregation ought to be magisterial, or convivial, or a devotional sanctuary. Those conflicting images often lurk just beneath the surface of the conflicts and tensions that periodically arise in the local church.

It is conceivable that the historical study of the congregation could provide the minister with the conceptual skills to recognize such images and to understand how they affect relationships within the church. It is also conceivable that such a minister could help the congregation itself understand not only the sources and history of the dominant images that govern its activities but also the unspoken assumptions that underlie those images.

One should not overlook the simple truth that congregations have histories and that the historical study of the congregation can at least make ministers and laypersons sensitive to some of the implications of that simple truth. Human beings bear their pasts throughout their lives. So do religious congregations, and the minister who fails to respect the particular history that has formed a congregation will almost invariably miss some important occasions for ministry. We have not been remarkably successful in convincing our students that "thinking historically" is a useful aid to ministry in a congregation. It is possible that historical investigation that takes the congregation as its object could engender a way of thinking about the local church that ministers would find valuable.

The current interest in the history of the congregation represents, finally, the logical next step for the social historians of religion who have attempted to recover patterns of thought and behavior that earlier scholars overlooked. It provides a means of moving closer to the grass roots and testing some of the grand abstractions—like secularization and modernization—that historians and social scientists have often used to interpret religious change in America. By helping us look closely at patterns of religious life that we have largely ignored, the study of the congregation promises to alter our vision of the history of religion in America.

PASTORAL CARE AND THE STUDY OF THE CONGREGATION

Don S. Browning

What would it mean to shift the focus in pastoral care from the minister to the congregation itself as the agent of care? And what would this change of focus mean for theological education for pastoral care? I must confess that before doing the research reported in this paper, I did not anticipate the conviction that I now hold: that this shift of focus makes a great difference, both for our understanding of pastoral care and for the way that pastoral care should be taught.

James Hopewell pushed us to consider altering the basic focus of theological education, to move away from what Edward Farley called the "clerical paradigm" to concern with the maturation of the congregation as the center of theological education. I believe that the most creative aspect of Hopewell's proposal was the suggestion that theological inquiry should begin with the descriptive—almost ethnologically descriptive—task of showing how "church and world are in fact instantiated in a particular place, what forms the historical and ecumenical context of a local church, . . . what constitutes its human situation and informs its response as a church."[1] I shall interpret these words to mean that all good practical theological thinking and acting should contain careful and detailed descriptions of the concrete empirical reality of the ministry's context. Hopewell understood this context first to be the local congregation, and it was from this perspective that I did my research. But the broader value of his admonition is using it to recognize the importance of "thick" descriptions of current practices as a prerequisite for the practical theological goals of any ministry, even the ministry in the context of the local congregation. Using Hopewell's challenge as my guide, I began a reconnaissance of the actual practices of care in a local congregation. I did this believing that such a description should not be an end in itself but an important early step in any practical theology of congregational care. My own commitments to a revisionist approach to practical theology require me to offer a hermeneutical description of actual practices in any ministerial context and to consider this task as seriously as the hermeneutic phe-

---

[1] See James Hopewell, "A Congregational Paradigm for Theological Education," earlier in this volume.

nomenology of the classic resources that would inform the norms of practice.[2]

It was shocking to me to have to admit that neither I nor the other
authors of the current literature of pastoral care (or what I prefer to call "the
practical theology of care") had ever attempted to describe what congregations actually do in their care for both their own members and the
people in their surroundings. Indeed, the literature has few descriptions of
what even ministers do in their pastoral care. Although the literature has
addressed the individual minister and suggested how care should be given, it
has seldom included descriptions of what actually is being done. Because of
this oversight, much of the contemporary literature on pastoral care must be
judged as one-sided and extremely narrow. It addresses only a small portion
of what either ministers or congregations actually do to provide care and
counsel for themselves and others.

A Profile of the Contemporary Pastoral Care Message

The significance of what I learned about actual congregational practices
is more striking if contrasted with what the standard pastoral care literature
actually recommends. First, the models of pastoral care found in the literature have been greatly influenced by the one-to-one and small-group practices of the modern psychotherapies. Pastoral care tends to refer to how the
minister can help individuals or small groups handle the problems of living
and growing spiritually. The emphasis has been on what the minister does.
Taking its cue from the modern secular psychotherapies, pastoral care has
advocated nonmoralistic listening, which is viewed as the core of the caring
process. In some instances, as with Seward Hiltner, this listening was used to
uncover submerged feelings that, if confronted and accepted, would give
troubled persons more strength to cope with their problems.[3] In other cases,
this nonmoralistic listening enabled the minister to make more sensitive
pastoral diagnoses that would then equip the minister to make more useful
and more accurate recommendations. Such a process is portrayed in Howard
Clinebell's earlier "revised model" of pastoral counseling.[4] There also has
been an increasing emphasis on "growth groups" as central to the minister's
care.[5] Indeed, the recent literature has concentrated on the congregation as

[2] See Don Browning, "Pastoral Theology in a Pluralistic Age," in *Practical Theology*, ed. Don
Browning (San Francisco: Harper & Row, 1983), 193; and also Don Browning, *Religious Ethics
and Pastoral Care* (Philadelphia: Fortress Press, 1983), 51.

[3] Seward Hiltner, *Pastoral Counseling* (Nashville: Abingdon Press, 1949), 97.

[4] Howard Clinebell, *Basic Types of Pastoral Care and Counseling* (Nashville: Abingdon Press,
1984), 10. I should point out that Clinebell has recently been moving toward a new model of
care that he calls the "holistic liberation-growth model." See pp. 25–46 of the 1984 edition of
Basic Types.

[5] Howard Clinebell, *Contemporary Growth Therapies* (Nashville: Abingdon Press, 1981).

the context of the pastor's care[6] and some works even give instructions for the training of laypersons in the skills of pastoral care and counseling.[7] But much of this literature seems only to extend the specialized atmosphere of much of the pastoral counseling literature to include elites of lay assistants who both imitate and support the minister's more specialized skills.[8] None of this literature takes seriously the task of actually describing what churches do to provide care and what the professional minister does to support and facilitate this larger congregational care.

Practical Theology and "Thick" Description

I am now convinced that theological education would be better if it taught students how to describe the ministry's various situations, including the local church. Such descriptions, however, must be "thick" and must cover the situation's symbolic, ethical, motivational, and social realities. Such a description might be called a hermeneutic-phenomenological description of current practices converging in ministerial situations. But I would emphasize the particular model of hermeneutical phenomenology associated with the work of Paul Ricoeur and David Tracy, in contrast with that associated with the work of Martin Heidegger and Hans-Georg Gadamer.[9] I mean to stress the more powerful hermeneutic phenomenology that also contains an explanatory moment and can therefore use the powerful explanatory tools of the modern human sciences such as psychology and sociology. Hence, to describe situations—even the situation of the local church—one should move through the full cycle of "understanding-explanation-understanding" along the lines that Ricoeur and Tracy advocated.[10]

When describing situations in this way, one approaches what Clifford Geertz called "thick description."[11] But in borrowing this phrase from Geertz, I shall not try to remain faithful to his special understanding of it. I agree, with Geertz, that thick description is primarily an effort to grasp the interrelations of different levels of signification in particular local cultural practices.[12] But because I intend to use description to help assess and

---

[6] See Diane Detwiler-Zapp and William Dixon, *Lay Caregiving* (Philadelphia: Fortress Press, 1981).

[7] Clinebell, *Basic Types*, 373–394.

[8] Clinebell, *Basic Types*, 373–394.

[9] Paul Ricoeur, "What Is a Text? Explanation and Understanding," *Hermeneutics and the Human Sciences* (London: Cambridge University Press, 1981), 145–164; David Tracy, *The Analogical Imagination* (New York: Crossroad, 1981), 117–118.

[10] See also Tracy's emphasis on a hermeneutic phenomenology for the interpretation of both common human experience and the Christian fact, in *Blessed Rage for Order* (New York: Seabury Press, 1978), 47–52.

[11] Clifford Geertz, *The Interpretation of Cultures* (New York: Basic Books, 1973), 6.

[12] Geertz, *The Interpretation of Cultures*, 10.

perhaps alter aspects of such practice, I propose using categories of analysis that can also be used for practical theology.

In recent writings I suggested five dimensions or levels of practical theological thinking.[13] In this essay, I shall use these five dimensions to guide the thick description of a congregation whose patterns of care I studied.

Practical theological thinking has (1) a visional or metaphorical level, (2) an obligational level, (3) a tendency-need level, (4) a contextual level, and (5) a rule-role level. In recent writings I used the word *dimension* in place of the word *level* to communicate that in actual praxis, these aspects of practical thinking are indeed woven together into the thickness of experience. But these different dimensions can be distinguished. Furthermore, the concept of levels is useful to communicate that the higher levels—for instance, the metaphorical and the obligational—exercise an important orienting influence on the lower levels of practical moral thinking. Yet the levels are quasi-autonomous in that fresh judgments are made at each level and the higher levels do not dictate in all respects the content of the lower levels.

First, all practical thinking assumes visions of the real world. These visions are communicated by means of stories and metaphors that convey images of the ultimate context of experience. Second, sometimes embedded in these visions and metaphors, but sometimes relatively independent, are implicit or explicit general principles of obligation. Examples of these can be found in the principle of neighbor love, the Golden Rule, or, perhaps, in Kant's categorical imperative or in the principle of utility. That there is some flexibility between the visional dimension and the obligational dimension of practical theological thinking can be seen in the fact that different cultures sometimes have similar general principles of obligation, even though they are animated and valorized by different ontological visions of the real world. Third, practical theological thinking assumes criteria of what humans want and need. Although these wants and needs are seldom immediately converted into morally justified goods, they do constitute indices of nonmoral goods that are further adjudicated by principles of obligation articulated at the second level. Fourth, practical thinking assumes some view or analysis of the context of praxis and particularly of how the pressures of the context help fulfill, distort, or limit the moral adjudication of the fundamental human needs assumed at the third level. And finally, after implicit or explicit judgments are made at all these levels, patterns of rules and roles guiding practical action are established by communities to order their life together. Of course, in most instances, we do not actually rethink our morality, nor should we; we simply rely, instead, on the practical moral wisdom of a

---

[13] Browning, *Religious Ethics and Pastoral Care*, 53–71; see also the application of these five levels or dimensions to integrating the various perspectives used to study the congregation, in *Building Effective Ministry*, ed. Carl Dudley (San Francisco: Harper & Row, 1983), 220–238.

particular tradition of praxis. But in transitions and crises, in which the wisdom of particular traditions is unsure or must be reinterpreted, we become more aware of these five dimensions and the need critically to realign them so as to address the prevailing issues.

The Study of a Congregation

Practical theological thinking fills these five dimensions with critically derived Christian content, especially at the first three levels. But in this study, I shall use these five dimensions to make a thick description of the care practices of a local congregation. It is my hope, however, that using the same categories for description that are also used for a critical practical theology will enhance the directive and transformative power of practical theological reflection.

Congregational Care in the Activist Church

The church that I chose to study is a liberal, socially activist church located near a major university. Twenty years ago the church was nearly dead. It attracted only 40 to 50 people for worship and had trouble paying its bills. But two social activist ministers turned the church around. The current minister, although socially active, has also developed a rich yet flexible liturgical tradition that emphasizes classical and folk forms of music, intelligent but informal sermons, liturgical dancing, and a warm and sometimes moving period when individuals can express themselves in a liturgical component called the "concerns of the people." Attendance currently ranges between 150 to 200. The church now sponsors a youth service center, a restaurant on its premises, and an intergenerational "covenantal community" made up of church members who live in a building on the edge of the slums and who attempt to serve that community. The church has recently become a "sanctuary church" and will soon vote to become a "nuclear-free zone." These latest actions evolved out of a two-year foreign policy study group that meets on Sunday morning and again for Tuesday breakfast.

To support my own interviews of the ministers and lay people of University Place, I also asked members of a small class of ministry students to study the churches to which they were assigned for their field education. I shall thus refer to my students' research to amplify some of the insights that emerged from my own interviews.

My initial impressions of this research suggest that (1) the minister's pastoral care is only a small part of the total care of a congregation; (2) members generally find more meaningful the informal care that they receive from one another than the care that they receive from their minister; (3) the members nonetheless expect and appreciate the minister's care during crises, transitions, and milestones of life; (4) some very caring ministers do relatively little individual counseling and, instead, spend more time facilitating the natural patterns of care that emerge in healthy congregations; and (5) although the skill of listening is indeed, as the literature indicates, the core of the minister's care, of equal importance are the skills of identifying the gifts and needs of individual members and creating networks of what Mansell Pattison called natural "psychosocial kinship groups" which he believes should be formed within and guided by the church's symbols and ethics.[14] When compared with the image of pastoral care found in most of the contemporary literature on the subject, these five impressions make a rather striking contrast.

Rules and Roles

For my study of University Place, I interviewed the senior minister, the minister to the students, a young layman in his early thirties, and an older laywoman in her sixties. My students also interviewed between three and four people in their churches, both ministers and laypersons. We began our interviews with the fifth dimension of practical theological thinking, the rule-role dimension, to uncover the basic patterns of care actually used in the congregations we studied. We started our interviews with the questions, What are the actual patterns of care that exist in this congregation? What do the members and the minister feel they should do and actually translate into action?

At University Place there was considerable congruence between the perceptions of the ministers and lay people of what was being done. They all listed the youth service and convenantal community as two important forms of "care for the world" that the church supported. But both the ministers and the lay people became more animated when they talked about the patterns of care within the congregation. Here care seemed to fall into the following patterns: (1) care in, by, and from formal groups; (2) care in, by, and from informal friendship groups; and (3) professional ministerial care given at the time of life-cycle transitions (birth, adolescence, marriage, illness, and death), individual pastoral counseling, and actual social service.

Care stemming from formal and informal groups elicited the most comment by both ministers and laypersons. The mutual support created by the long-standing foreign policy study group was mentioned frequently and, to a lesser degree, the spontaneous care and mutual support that accompanied many other committees and working groups in the church. But the care evolving from the informal networks evoked the most comment by everyone. The senior pastor illustrated this by telling about the network of young couples in the church, that is, their custom of passing around to expectant couples a handmade cradle belonging to an older member of the church and

---

[14] E. Mansell Pattison, *Pastor and Parish—A Systems Approach* (Philadelphia: Fortress Press, 1977), 18.

their passing from couple to couple sacks of clothes for the pregnant mother and the newborn infant—clothes that would later be lent to another young family.

Both the senior minister and the minister of students admitted that they spent much time encouraging such groups. The two lay people, especially the young man (whose wife was herself pregnant), admitted that these informal groups were to them the most important aspect of the congregation's care. The truly "warm moments," the moments that "kept them coming" and "keep them going," came from these groups. Indeed, these groups were more important to this young activist couple (the husband is the congregational authority on the ethics of nuclear deterrence) than was anything that the ministers themselves did in their care. This view was shared by many of the lay people interviewed by my students. One layman in a large urban congregation put it this way: "I don't have much personal contact with the ministers, but I don't mind this. The care and concern between the members of my Sunday class is what is really important."

But there was an exception to this. In University Place it was clear to the senior minister that the pastors must be present and participate in the major crises and transitions of life. The pastor's presence during times of illness and life-cycle transition is extremely important. It is long remembered by church members and helps consolidate the bond between the minister and the layperson in ways that carry over into many other relations. The church's liturgical functions enacted at these times of transition were viewed by the two ministers of University Place as fundamental to pastoral care, and there was remarkable congruence on this point between the ministers and the two laypersons. According to the older woman, "This is a busy church, even what might be called a 'hot church.' The ministers don't have to be available all the time as long as they are available at the right time."

University Place found that its informal patterns of care grew rather spontaneously, although the senior minister admitted doing a "lot of internal referring" of people to one another and to these groups. Not all churches that my students examined had these groups or created them as spontaneously. The people in one church seemed to be rather mistrustful of one another, and accordingly, spontaneous "kinship groups" were less common. In the larger urban churches, the associate ministers helped create and maintain caring and visitation groups. These associate and assistant ministers worried about the overwhelming numbers of people to care for, about "people falling through the cracks." They recognized the necessity of rationalizing and systematizing the congregation's care and yet resented that creating such groups and training lay people to give care could sometimes keep the ministers at a distance from the primary work of care. The lay peole themselves, however, seemed not to worry about this as long as ordained ministerial presence, symbolic power, and liturgical sensitivity were manifest at the grand moments of life.

Individual and small-group counseling occupies a relatively small portion of time for both of the ministers of University Place. The senior minister limits his pastoral counseling to three sessions, although some people simply "drop in for a conversation every few months." The pastors that my students interviewed said much the same thing. They all agreed that "nonmoralistic listening and empathy" were the heart of care but that the structured counseling relationship was only a small part of this care. The exception to this was the larger congregations in which the pressure to provide some form of structured pastoral counseling intensified in proportion to the difficulty of establishing informal or formal networks of care and support. All of this suggests that individual pastoral counseling in the education of prospective ministers should not be overemphasized.

The Contextual Dimension of Care

Congregational care at University Place is shaped in part by how it interprets its sociological contexts. The fact that it is located in an interracial community, near a large and powerful university, all of which is surrounded by sprawling urban slums affects its care. But the important point is how these facts are interpreted. The prevailing interpretation is as follows: The interracial community is genuinely affirmed (the church is now about 20 percent black); the university's intellectual ideals are affirmed, but with some ambivalence; and the almost overwhelming urban problems are viewed as exasperating but as opportunities for ministry (for example, the youth service and the covenantal community). The church's own members and to some extent the larger community regards the church as existing in a state of intense activity, launching projects on nearly all fronts, debating and discussing and trying to be judicious in its commitments, but becoming overheated all the same.

University Place wants simultaneously to be a close-knit family and to have an intense social ministry. The deeper it goes with the latter, the more important becomes the former. But the quest to become a family seemed to be a widespread goal of at least two-thirds of my students' churches as well. But no matter how intensely this need was felt, it took different forms, depending not so much on the context itself but on the way that a particular church interpreted its context. Different slogans reflecting the image of the family characterized the various churches. Care at University Place was "supporting the activism of the family of God." But a declining suburban church was equally interested in being a family. But because it viewed its situation as basically hopeless, its care was more a matter of "maintaining the family of God." Another recently established upper-middle-class suburban church characterized its care as "creating the family of God." The professional staff of a large, successful, and wealthy inner-city congregation viewed itself as hoping to "discover and enhance the inner core of the family of God," a core that might care for the larger anonymous membership. A new

Asian congregation saw itself as "establishing the family of God." Pastoral care in this last church was strongly directive and instrumental and helped settle, employ, feed, and establish a new immigrant people in Chicago's urban wilds. Other churches, however, did not seem to have the drive to become a family. In these churches, care tended to be primarily pastoral, what the ministers did to show concern and attention to the troubled people of the congregation, with relatively little assistance from the larger congregation. What struck me as I compared my study with those of my students was how important the sociological context was to determining a church's care and how even more important the church's interpretation of the context was.

Tendencies and Needs

At this level of practical theological thinking, we need to survey both psychobiological wants and needs and those other needs that appear to be almost completely the products of religiocultural definition. In addition to the basic needs of food and clothing, to which University Place attended in its food pantry program, its rummage sales, and its general benevolence giving (which, by the way, was not as high as one would expect for an activist church), the greatest single need voiced by both lay people and ministers was the problem of loneliness, especially the loneliness associated with urban academic communities. The graduate students were lonely; the professional men and women had fewer intimate friends than they needed; and the older people were isolated and forgotten. This loneliness led to the creation of formal and informal "kinship groups." In addition to the one for young couples, one of the most important of these was the so-called Epiphany Clusters, which met weekly during the winter. These were neighborhood intergenerational groups that gathered for dinner at a member's home and spent several weeks studying such topics as Central America, the Soviet Union, or the Middle East.

But the senior minister mentioned other, related needs that were unique to the care of University Place. Graduate students needed a place to explore wider aspects of themselves than they were permitted to reveal in their studies. Middle-aged professionals needed a context in which they could reveal more of themselves than their professions required. The minister of students and the young layman commented that everyone needed to "slow up" and to learn that "we don't have to do it all ourselves."

But here a real tension began to emerge in University Place—a tension between the care needs of the activists, who included a significant portion of the congregation, and the care needs of those members who were neither activists nor articulate about their own pains. There also may have been a crisis in the church's ethics of care between its obligations to the needs of the activists "who get tired and sometimes uncertain" and its obligations to those who did not have the strength or skills to communicate their hurts to others.

As the minister of students asserted, "We can handle Jim (a young man with drug-induced brain damage) and Cindy (a highly medicated emotionally disturbed woman), but I worry about the persons who can't gain attention for themselves." So far, no special strategy has been developed to address this problem, only the hope that somehow the existing networks are catching most of these people.

The minister articulated another set of "needs" related to his own theological vision for University Place: "People here need to take themselves less seriously at University Place. We encourage social responsibility, but it is important for us never to say that there is something a person *has to do*. I try to make certain that no single vision of "righteousness" becomes dominant here—becomes absolutized. These people are so busy; they push themselves so hard." And the minister described how sin usually was expressed in University Place: It took the form of "people taking themselves too seriously in almost every aspect of their lives—in their schoolwork, in their professions, in their church responsibilities. They are always putting such high demands on themselves. I try to make certain I do nothing to deepen this tendency. And indeed, there is an element of self-righteousness in it all as well."

The way that the churches' central pastoral care needs were interpreted and defined varied among the churches studied by my students. One church defined itself predominantly in response to the needs of its older people. Another church concentrated on the needs of the younger, upwardly mobile families. The newly established Asian church defined the needs of its members mainly as their needs for jobs, homes, language training, and assistance. The minister himself was the central agent for meeting these needs. He functioned as translator, financial adviser, job placement broker, and marriage counselor and did all of this with a firmness and authority that would have been incomprehensible in the middle-class white urban and suburban churches. The problem of urban loneliness was central to the care needs of the large inner-city urban congregation but was compounded by an equal degree of reluctance by most of its members to be imposed on by either the church staff or other members. Another large suburban church tried to meet the basic needs of the ill and the bereaved. But outside this, this church expected the professional staff to spot those needs among its members that the congregation itself might not detect. And as was the case with University Place, distortions of the spirit, sins, and idolatries took different forms from church to church.

The Obligational Level

The question about the ethics of care seemed strange to some of the people interviewed by my students and me. But generally, after a bit of reflection, answers began to flow. At University Place, questions about the ethics of care centered on "who was being left out." The older laywoman wondered who—if not her and her husband—would cart the elderly back and forth to church, call them, and make sure that they were generally all right. University Place has a coterie of older people whom the rest of the church tends to regard with admiration, interest, and concern. But there are others less commanding in their personal presence or too ill or isolated to gain such attention. Sometimes both members and staff are stricken with guilt when they realize that someone has not been called, seen, or heard from for several months. All four of the people that I interviewed worried about whether this had happened more than they realized. They admitted it was clearly a question of the ethics of care.

Other interesting and subtle ethical issues also were discussed. The senior minister volunteered that he offered ethical suggestions in his pastoral counseling but that he never invoked the authority of God or the church for concrete suggestions; he always presented them as his personal point of view. The minister of students and the young layman were clearly concerned with the limits of care, as indeed was the senior minister. They all seemed to believe that the church should not, in its care, swamp the agency and dignity of those for whom it cared. The senior minister admitted, "We can never take total responsibility." And the minister to students was concerned about how to communicate appropriate boundaries for the church's care. "Because we cannot care for everyone, who are we primarily responsible for, and how can we communicate this to others? And how, once we define our limits, can we work with sectors of the community to ensure that those who are beyond our energies are indeed being attended to by someone?" In University Place we found a church that may have been trying to do more than it could, but it was also a church working to discover the ethical grounds for limiting itself.

The ethical grounds may have been emerging from the surprising amount of ethical talk I heard that moral theologians would classify under the heading of "ethics of caritas" or "ethics of mutuality."[15] The young layman believed that everyone in the church needed to be more open to receive care and assistance from others. He was, again, especially concerned with bring-ing a calming influence to the "frantic activity" which, he readily confessed, he was equally guilty of himself. "University Place may not do well by people with particularly maternal needs, and it may be that we all should be open to receiving a little more maternal care than we admit we need." But the senior minister himself was the most involved in developing an ethic of caritas to guide the church's care. "It is important to remind myself that in addition to my responsibility to care for others, they have a responsibility to care for me. I am learning this only slowly." In response to my question about the role of agape in Christian care, he responded, "Certainly we must take the first step, reach out, even sacrifice, but that should not be the permanent state of

---

[15] For a discussion of the caritas tradition, see Anders Nygren, *Agape and Eros* (Philadelphia: Westminster Press, 1953), 449–563.

affairs. We must let the situation return to mutuality as soon as possible." I asked him if he were saying that agape as self-sacrificial love was transitional to the restoration of mutuality, and he answered, "Yes, that is the way that I *want* to see it, but it has taken me many years to understand that sacrificial love is necessary but still not the final and exclusive goal of Christian care."[16]

The churches in which my students interviewed had various ways of characterizing their ethics of care. The ethics of exclusion and inclusion was, in different forms, a widespread concern. (Who was being left out or excluded and why?) One church was concerned with the ethics of "handling its many social misfits and its street people." The ethics of confidentiality was also a common concern. The Asian church dealt with its ethical issues "on a scriptural model." One minister saw the ethics of care as basically "knowing when to criticize and when to affirm." I left my own interviews, and I think the students left theirs, feeling that little solid work was being done by either ministers or their churches to clarify the ethical foundations of the focus, breadth, and limits of their congregational care.

The Visional and Metaphorical Dimensions

The visional or metaphorical dimensions of practical theological thinking are the most influential. They are the source of our final interpretation of the possibilities of life and the world. They shape—but do not determine in all respects—the lower levels of practical thinking. But these dimensions' ability to orient both thought and behavior can, I think, be easily discerned in congregational care in general and in the care of University Place in particular. Several churches are located within a short walking distance of University Place. They serve much the same community, contain many of the same socioeconomic classes of people, and see and live with one another in the same neighborhood. But even the most superficial observation indicates that each of these churches has a different religioethical vision and culture, and their practical congregational lives have different emphases. Two of these other churches were among those that my students examined, and their own studies added evidence to these casual observations.

The senior minister of University Place used the metaphor of "hopeful exploring" to summarize his role in the care of his congregation:

> A congregation with a strong social mission needs to maintain
> its hope. In many ways, the world situation is not going well
> from the standpoint of the commitments of University Place. I
> need to project a vision of life that celebrates the continued
> presence and activity of God. But I have to do this in a

---

[16]The position toward which the pastor seemed headed was well stated by Louis Janssens, "Norms and Priorities in a Love Ethics," *Louvain Studies* 6 (Spring 1977): 207–238. It also seems close to the concept of equal regard developed by Gene Outka, *Agape* (New Haven, Conn.: Yale University Press, 1972), 260–274.

> modality of exploration. We don't always know the right thing
> to do. In my care and counseling with individuals, I often don't
> know the right thing to do. I don't provide the answers, but I
> assume that some actions and attitudes are better than others
> and that relatively good answers can be found—hence, the
> reason for "hopeful exploring."

This metaphor seemed to suggest a theology of God's ongoing creative activity (*creatio continua*) that would someday culminate in the fulfillment of the human community.

The minister to students used the metaphorical expressions of Matthew 25:34: "I was hungry and you gave me food, I was thirsty and you gave me drink . . ." as these are used in scripture to relate the hungry and thirsty to the person of Christ. These metaphorical expressions seemed to ground this minister's concern with "those who are being left out or who are getting tired and dropping behind." Both laypersons mentioned the metaphor of the shepherd, but the young layman added that "shepherds must remember that they are also sheep, and sheep must be helped to become shepherds." And then he went on to say that "at University Place we are aware of the shepherding aspects of care, but it is very difficult for us to admit to being sheep. Yet we need to depend on each other more than we do; we need to be aware of our limits." It is interesting to note that this young layman was a prime mover in introducing prayer and meditation at the beginning and end of the foreign policy study group's Sunday and Tuesday meetings, a marked departure from the style of a church that no more than two years ago would have impressed the casual visitor as distinctively unpious, even secular.

The leaders interviewed at University Place seemed acutely aware of the paradoxes of care in an activist church predominantly composed of individuals who were also busy students, professors, schoolteachers, and other professionals. The distortions of the spirit that tempted this church moved toward self-righteousness, Prometheanism, frantic activity, elitism, and a sense of despair and gloom when cherished goals seemed unrealizable. More recently, a warm and rich worship life, an increasingly prayerful and meditative attitude toward its study and action, and a growing sense of not wanting "to add more burdens than necessary" became features of this church's ethos, and they appear to be able to deal with its deepening engagements with the world. All of this seemed to flow from metaphors of ultimacy that emphasize God's continuing presence and directive action, a need for openness and a joint inquiry to determine right action, and the need for mutuality in care and spirituality.

Theological Education, Care, and Congregational Studies

The new interest in congregational studies correlates with the similarly recent revival of interest in the nature of practical theology. But the two movements are not identical in their commitments. Both movements try to include yet go beyond what Edward Farley called the "clerical paradigm."[17] But they surpass the clerical paradigm in different ways. For the most part, the practical theology movement has attempted to broaden the definition of practical theology beyond theological reflection on the professional acts and roles of the ordained minister[18] in order to include critical theological reflection on all aspects of the norms of practice of the church in the world.[19] The congregational studies program wants to go beyond the clerical para-digm and emphasize the culture and practice of the congregation as a whole. By contrast, the practical theology movement aims to reflect all aspects of the practice of the church in the world—the congregation being only one, albeit crucial, aspect of the church's activity.

Hence, from the perspective of these newer visions of practical theology, the emphasis of congregational studies must be seen as both welcome and limited. It is welcome because it has helped us take seriously the need to describe the richness of congregations in all their empirical facticity. It is limited in that it has not yet spelled out the role of this kind of description in the context of the larger task of critical practical theological reflection.[20] The study and description of congregations must be seen as an important but neglected aspect of practical theological reflection and action on congrega-tional life. But there are other contexts of Christian action that also must be studied and described with equal care, and the place of these descriptions must be worked out as part of a critical practical theology.

In other writings, I have argued that a revised correlational approach to practical theology will prove to be the most faithful and productive for the needs of Christian practice within the context of modern, pluralistic so-cieties. In this report, I have demonstrated some of the richness of under-standing that can be gained from students and faculty making careful descriptions of the churches they propose to serve. I have suggested that this description will be more helpful if the same categories used for practical theological reflection are also used for the actual description of the church. This would facilitate the turn from description to actual theological prescrip-

---

[17] Edward Farley, *Theologia: The Fragmentation and Unity of Theological Education* (Phila-delphia: Fortress Press, 1983), 87–88.

[18] This was the position of most of the authors in Browning, ed., *Practical Theology*. See specifically p. 10.

[19] See Farley's amplification of this point regarding his critique of the old fourfold pattern of theological education. Does the Hopewell proposal leave us within the fourfold model? Farley, *Theologia*, 141–151.

[20] None of the articles in Dudley's *Building Effective Ministry* attempted this, with the exception of my own, "Integrating the Approaches: A Practical Theology," 220–237. This may have been because in this project I was assigned that task. But I did notice that throughout the development of the project, there was little explicit interest in determining the place of congregational studies within the larger theological enterprise.

tion. It also would mean submitting the current theories and practices at each of these five levels to a new hermeneutical consideration of the normative images of the church found in the tradition and to a new theological consideration of the fundamental visions and metaphors, broad ethical principles, and basic definitions of human need that the tradition offers. It would then mean a mutual correlation and criticism of these levels of practical thinking with the prevailing practices in the community being studied. In some instances, these practices can be affirmed as relatively faithful but still needing deepening, enriching, or cleansing. In other instances, they will need radical renewal. But in either case, criticism and change can come with more sensitivity and realism and a greater sense of both the necessary and the possible next steps to take if balanced with better descriptions of the current practices of the church being addressed.

I shall conclude by listing some of the benefits that I believve that both faculty and students gained from this congregational description of pastoral care.

> 1. I believe that we broadened our understanding of what congregations do in their caring ministries. This exercise exposed the narrowness of the bias toward pastoral counseling in much of the literature and teaching in recent years.

> 2. This description made us aware of the different churches' various ecologies of care and the range of skills and tasks that different situations require.

> 3. This description demonstrated the importance (more forcefully than does the contemporary pastoral care literature) of the minister's personal, symbolic, and liturgical presence in the great transitions of life. It also suggested the importance of having normative theological models for understanding these transitions. This study did not uncover such models, but had it done so, they would have needed further theological reflection to determine their relative adequacy.

> 4. This description suggested that the most meaningful part of care from the perspective of lay people is what they receive from one another in the informal and formal groups making up the ongoing life of the congregation. In some instances these groups can be highly task oriented, such as the foreign policy study group at University Place.

> 5. Finally, this description suggested that the minister's additional contribution to congregational care is his or her ability to facilitate the caring dimension of these formal and informal groups and to establish a commanding theology and ethics within which the groups can understand and gain sanction for what they do.

In summary, I reiterate my argument that congregational studies must be viewed as only one aspect of the larger task of practical theological thinking and action. As such, I believe they can—as I hope I have demonstrated in this case study—make an important contribution to the teaching of pastoral care in theological education.

THE MINISTRY OF A CONGREGATION: RETHINKING CHRISTIAN ETHICS FOR A CHURCH-CENTERED SEMINARY

Stanley Hauerwas

The Church and Christian Ethics

Those who use the same terms in religious conversations are in fact talking about quite different matters. Such a reminder is important to any attempt to rethink, and perhaps even reform, seminary education in relation to congregational life. It is also important to explaining, as I have been asked to do, how my field of study illuminates the actual culture of a local church and how, in turn, the life of that congregation may affect how I teach in a Master of Divinity program.[1] The problem with such rethinking—or explaining—is that almost everyone agrees it is an extremely good idea, an "idea whose time has come." The difficulty, however, is that words like *church* and *congregation* are so vague that our agreement may well mask deeper disagreements if we explore further what we mean by those terms.

For example, it took me some time to realize that when I say the word *church* to Roman Catholics, they understand something quite different from what I intended. Thus they often resist my oft-stated claim, "The church does not have a social ethic; the church is a social ethic," for reasons that I at

---

[1] Elsewhere in this volume, in "A Congregational Paradigm for Theological Education," James Hopewell expands on this assignment by suggesting a seminary's need for a

> fundamentally revised curriculum, different in both form and focus, that shifts theological education from a clerical to a congregational paradigm. The program's main object would be the development of the congregation, not of the student.
>
> The proposal is not necessarily a plea for more contextual or field education in the curriculum, or one that advocates a greater proportion of pastoral theology courses. Such measures by themselves cannot change a program's fix on the individual.
>
> . . . Instead, the proposal seeks an accomplishment deeper than a physical or political association. It aims to join seminary and congregation in a quest for the redemptive community. It gives to each partner the responsibilty, now consigned to the church in general, to pursue the means by which a particular group of human beings gathered in the name and power of Christ in fact work together to fulfill the Christian promise.

first did not grasp. I began to understand them only when I realized that for Roman Catholics, *church* suggests a complex hierarchical structure that culminates in Rome. Therefore my claim that the church is, rather than has, a social ethic can sound to Roman Catholic ears like a form of papal supremacy. I did not realize this partly because my understanding of *church* is determined by the small white frame building on the corner of Pleasant Mound Drive and Buckner Boulevard in Pleasant Grove, Texas, where my family went to hear Brother Russell preach and where sometimes after the service we had picnics in the graveyard behind the church. It was a long way from Rome.

Of course, theologians are supposed to know better than to allow such "pictures" of the church to determine their theology. Church, after all, is not a descriptive term but a theological claim about God's creation of a new people. It is also a theological issue regarding how the church's doctrine is to be correlated with the empirical church, but such an issue rarely seems to require the theologian to discuss what goes on in any actual community. My aim in this paper, however, is to counter this kind of abstractness insofar as I can explain how my field of study illumines the life of "a local church," but I am unsure with which local church I should begin.

Indeed, I am tempted to use this paper to develop my argument that the integrity of Christian ethics as a theological discipline requires a recovery of the significance of the church, but I would thereby continue to use *church* in a vague and unspecified way. If challenged that no one knows of an empirical church like the one for which I am calling, I could offer the ultimate theological "out," that my task as a theologian is not to say what the church is but what the church ought to be. Yet I cannot be happy with that response, as it seems to distinguish between the visible and invisible church in a way that I think is theologically untenable.

To avoid speaking only about an ideal church, I shall tell a story of an event in a congregation's life. I want to be candid, however, about the status of this narrative. I am sure it does not deserve to be regarded as, nor do I intend it to be, a case study.[2] Accordingly, I have not done the sociological or historical work required for that kind of enterprise. More important, however, is that my perspective is not sociological or anthropological but nor-

---

[2] To me, a case study is the cross-disciplinary approach found in Carl S. Dudley, ed., *Building Effective Ministry: Theory and Practice in the Local Church* (San Francisco: Harper & Row, 1983). However, I also do not want to be too modest about my using an example for the position I develop. I suspect that one of the reasons that theologians and seminary education ignore the life of the congregation is a correlate of the prejudice against examples for intellectual work since the Enlightenment. From such a perspective, examples at best are considered anecdotal and cannot have the status of evidence or knowledge. As a result, the nature and status of practical knowledge have been ignored, particularly in modern philosophy and theology. To make the congregation a central concern in seminary education, therefore, must be a new pedagogical strategy that requires the assumption that theology is from the beginning to the end a form of practical knowledge.

mative. My selection, as well as the way I have chosen to relate the event, is meant to be both an example and an argument for how Christian ethics should be practiced as well as how seminary curricula should be restructured if the congregation is to be taken seriously. My account is meant to be an example of the kind of church that seminaries should seek to serve, enrich, and, if necessary, help create.

Moreover, the way I tell the story of this church is obviously informed by my constructive theological and ethical interests and is also an attempt to test them. For example, one of the criticisms of my emphasis on the centrality of the church for Christian ethics is that it is insufficiently schooled by the empirical reality of the contemporary church. The kind of church for which I call does not exist and probably cannot exist, given our world's political and economic realities. Nonetheless, the church that I describe is real and has acted and is acting in a way that I think the church should. Another criticism is that my sense of the church is "sectarian," as my "ethic" would make it impossible for Christians to participate in the life of our society. Although I do not think that participation is good in itself, I hope that my narrative of how one church acted will explain why I think the alternatives of church-sect and withdrawal-participation are false.

Twenty years ago Langdon Gilkey stated that the great problem of American denominations is that they are a sect-type

> in Christendom, in culture. The separated community has become the community church, related inherently and intentionally to the world. This new form creates the present possibility of the transformation of the world of which it is now fully a part. Unhappily, it is also the source of most of our serious problems. As we have noted, this new form preserves no essential area separate or removed from cultural domination. Unlike the church-type, it has no sacred hierarchy, no holy sacraments, no holy dogmas; and yet, unlike the sects, it possesses no separated communal, moral, and intellectual life. Having no separate areas which might be able to preserve the holy *from* the world, and thus be enabled to mediate the holy *to* the world, this church is in fact in imminent danger of being engulfed by the world.[3]

[3] Langdon Gilkey, *How the Church Can Minister to the World Without Losing Itself* (New York: Harper & Row, 1964), 19–20. Gilkey argued that this analysis is true for most American religious groupings, as the various denominations in America—despite different histories, theologies, and governments—have come increasingly to resemble one another. Though notable exceptions could be named, I think Gilkey is generally right that the ethos of the white American Protestant congregation, irrespective of its formal allegiance, conforms to the denominational type. That is, perhaps, why the attempt to study the place of a congregation for seminary education without reference to denominational identity makes descriptive sense, although whether it can be justified normatively is another matter.

In short, the church in America is dying of its own success. As a sect it created a culture that in principle is built on freedom of religion, but to preserve that freedom the church now finds it necessary to underwrite rather than criticize the society that allegedly allows it to be free. Please do not misunderstand. I am not suggesting that religious freedom is a sham. Rather, I am suggesting that the church that is free is so because it does not threaten our society. This condition, moreover, applies to Christians of both the left and the right, as both tend to return to society baptised idealizations first learned from society itself.

For many in Christian ethics, the church is thus more of a problem than a resource for constructive theological reflection. Teachers of seminary ethics are more likely to affirm, at least in principle, a relationship between Christian ethics and participation in the church's ministry, but as Dieter Hessel observed, "ethics as taught in seminary still tends to view the ministering congregation as an *addendum* to the 'real subject matter' of biblical and theological ethics, philosophical and political theory, or social policy evaluation. Ethics as a discipline of biblical and systematic theology remains separated from exploration of ministry as a practical theological concern."[4] Thus we have created a situation in which the most pressing issue is how courses in theology and ethics can be made relevant to the ministry's actual work.

Tom Ogletree noted in his 1984 presidential address to the Society of Christian Ethics that most Christian ethicists do not see their task as providing moral guidance for Christian communities and congregations.

> [As a result] of powerful forces, such communities have come to have significance chiefly in the private sector, in relation to

---

[4] Dieter T. Hessel, "Christian Ethics and the Congregation's Social Ministry," *Annual of the Society of Christian Ethics, 1984*, ed. Larry Rasmussen (Waterloo, Ontario: Council on the Study of Religion, 1984), 45. Hessel suggested that though I reassert that the church is a distinct society with an alternative social vision, I am led to "some problematic social policy prescriptions which undergird a particular (conventional?) view of virtue and character" (p. 57). I have no idea what a "conventional view of virtue and character" might look like, but my argument was that it is quite unconventional for the church to be the kind of society that can encourage the growth of virtue and character.

In "The Revival of Practical Theology," *Christian Century* 101 (February 1–8, 1984), Don Browning made a similar charge. Noting that some may be tempted to construe Edward Farley's call in *Theologia* for theology again to become *habitus* and *paideia* in terms of the renewed interest in virtue and character, Browning stated that this would be a mistake. For the emphasis on virtue, according to Browning, lacks the character necessary to sustain the church's public ministry. He suggested that we "abstract from the Christian story a more identifiable set of principles and procedures which could be used in public debates over the country" (p. 136). Without arguing the point, I think this way of putting the matter cannot help but underwrite the divorce of seminary education—particularly in terms of ethics—from the life of the congregation.

families and residential neighborhoods. Given this confinement, they have had little direct access to the great social questions of the day. In many instances they have become places of escape from disturbing realities in modern society, encouraging nostalgic attachments to former ways of life, viewpoints, furnishing moral and religious justifications for advantaged classes, and abandoning the victims of social dislocation in rapidly changing environments. To put the point baldly, most of the Christian congregations we know first hand are not disposed to share the passion for social justice which many of us profess. They appear more interested in maintaining secure spaces which can sustain them in their attempts to cope with the daily problems of living.[5]

Yet Ogletree also argued that any constructive thinking in Christian ethics in the future will require an ecclesial context: "If we are to be interpreters of Christian ethics in our time, we will have to give fresh attention to the church as a community capable of sustaining a distinctive moral vision of the world."[6] The very community capable of sustaining that vision, however, seems to be what is missing. Christian ethics is thus often considered as a form of philosphical analysis rather than as a service in and for real people who bear the name church. That I think is the problem confronting Christian ethics and why so many who are trained in Christian ethics have difficulty taking the church seriously.

But like Ogletree, I believe we have no choice. We must take the church seriously if Christian ethics is to have something interesting to say about our society. For ironically, to the extent that Christian ethicists have abandoned the church because of its "suburban captivity," we have been unable to maintain our theological integrity.[7] My example is therefore meant to address these issues, for I hope to show that church is much more than a formal abstraction for Christian theological and ethical reflection.

[5]Thomas Ogletree, "The Ecclesial Context of Christian Ethics," *Annual of the Society of Christian Ethics, 1984*, ed. Larry Rasmussen (Waterloo, Ontario: Council on the Study of Religion, 1984), 4. There is no question of the descriptive power of Ogletree's observation, but the problem is not simply that congregations have become bastions of middle-class respectability. At least part of the problem is the ethicists' presumption that we know what "the great social questions of the day" are or that our passion for "social justice" is any less accommodationist than is the middle-class church. At least part of the reason for attending to the life of congregations for the development of Christian ethics is to consider that "attempts to cope with the daily problems of living" are a resource for recovering a more radical social stance of the church.

[6]Ogletree, "The Ecclesial Context of Christian Ethics," 10.

[7]For an account of Christian ethics that develops this point, see Stanley Hauerwas, "On Keeping Theological Ethics Theological," *Revisions: Changing Perspectives in Moral Philosophy*, ed. Stanley Hauerwas and Alasdair MacIntyre (Notre Dame, Ind.: University of Notre Dame Press, 1983), 16–42.

An Event in the Life of a Congregation

The event that I shall use as an example took place at an administrative board meeting of a local United Methodist church, no doubt one of the last places one might expect anything significant to happen. Moreover, most of the people at the board meeting that night probably thought it was a fairly routine meeting, but as a member of the board I was struck by what happened.

Broadway United Methodist Church is on the south side of South Bend, Indiana, three blocks from the town's main street, Michigan Avenue. It is in one of those sections of town with which we have become all too familiar, a neighborhood that began to "go down" about twenty years ago but has not quite reached bottom. Originally it was an area of town where many of the workers at the Studebaker plant lived. Though the houses were not impressive, they were comfortable two-story homes. In the early sixties, however, a city-planning decision was made to put a highway through a mainly black area of the city. Afterward, having little choice, poor black people began to rent in the area around Broadway. This process was accelerated by the closing of Studebaker and the subsequent loss of the neighborhood's economic base. More recently the neighborhood has been reintegrated, with many young couples moving back into the area, which provides reasonably priced housing. There is even a fairly active neighborhood association that has fought the nearby pornography stores as well as the prostitution trade centered on the corner of Broadway and Michigan—three blocks from the church.

The Broadway United Methodist Church has a fairly large building, which was constructed for its once big and lively congregation. It has a long history in South Bend, first housing an evangelical church established by German pietists. The congregation then affiliated with the Evangelical United Brethren Church and moved to the south side of town, where most of its members live.[8]

Acknowledging Where We Are

The congregation of the church now numbers about one hundred, with the average Sunday attendance averaging between forty to sixty. The loss of members can be attributed to several factors. The closing of Studebaker certainly helped reduce the congregation, though many in the church remained extraordinarily loyal: Even after they moved, some continued to drive a good distance to return to the church for worship. But the integration of the church in the early sixties, coupled with a series of disastrous pastors, nearly closed the church's doors. No doubt the church was viewed as having

---

[8] However, the church has always had many members who lived a good distance away.

a questionable future by denominational executives, as given the surrounding neighborhood, there seemed to be little chance of recovery.

In the early seventies, however, a pastor was appointed to the church who simply refused to give up. He was given the appointment because he was coming back into the North Indiana conference from California and thus was given a "problem" church. What was a problem for others, however, was an exciting possibility for him. By visiting the sick, organizing the church, and helping develop an urban ministry, the pastor enabled the congregation to gain a new sense of confidence in their value to one another and, in particular, to the neighborhood. When I joined the church in the late seventies, I found a group of committed people determined to do much more than just survive[9]—they were determined to be present as the church on the southeast side, battling any person or institution that hinted they should give up. Moreover, the congregation was extremely heterogeneous in race, age, economic background, and education.

The board meeting I shall describe took place about four years ago. The first item on the agenda was the leaky roof over the education building. This addition to the church was its last great project before the decline. Because we no longer had enough members to have a full Sunday school, the education building was now used mainly by the Head-Start program, for which the church was the primary administrator. Therefore we had to consider repairs on a part of the building that housed a program that many churches would not have considered integral to the life of the church.

We had gotten estimates, and it turned out that the repairs would be quite extensive if the job were done right. It was going to cost us at least $5,000 for a new roof, a huge sum for our church. The board had a lengthy discussion of the various bids, considering such matters as which company had the best reputation and what kind of roof would last the longest. The

[9] How I became a member at Broadway is a tale in itself, but I was at least initially attracted by a challenge from the pastor. After I had given a talk at a continuing education seminar for United Methodist clergy of the conference, he had the nerve to ask me (in the bathroom at that) where I went to church. After I explained that I tended to bounce around, he suggested that I was not living out the theological claims I professed. I figured that anyone who challenged me in that way could not be all bad. After attending the church for some time and deciding to join, I was a bit taken aback when he would not allow me to join the church unless I went through weekly membership classes for six months—from his perspective I might have known a lot about theology, but that did not mean I knew much about what it meant to be a member of this church. I learned.

The way I tell this story may give the impression that the pastor is the central figure in the story of Broadway. That is certainly not the case, as he would be the first to say. In fact, after reading the first draft of this paper, he insisted that I say that he in many ways followed the congregation's lead. For example, the decision to stick it out in the neighborhood was made before his arrival. Indeed, it was not so much that they "made a decision" about that but, rather, that they were just not the kind of people that give up easily. I regret that I lack the space and the skill to depict the character of many of the members of the church, of which the pastor was only one.

board finally voted to accept the most expensive bid because it seemed the best.

To me, what was remarkable about this discussion and decision was what was not discussed. No one suggested that we rethink the investment, given our situation in the neighborhood. No one proposed that we instead consider saving this money to relocate in the suburbs. Rather, they simply assumed that all the important moral commitments had been made and were no longer subject to debate. As a result, the decision to reroof was made in a businesslike way, with no one noticing that the church was going on record that it would rather be in this neighborhood than elsewhere.

But the neighborhood noticed. The machinery that pulled up to the church to do the reroofing signaled to the people of the neighborhood that they were not to be abandoned, at least not by this church. Some might have suggested that we not spend the money on the building but instead on more food for our food pantry, through which we gave food to anyone who asked for it. But that for us was not a real choice, as we first had to maintain the building if we were to show that we were committed to being present as God's people on the southeast side of South Bend, Indiana.

This point was made clear to us a little later. We had been providing a place for the "Faith Center," a predominantly black pentecostal church, to worship during the week and on Sunday. We had hoped this might lead to a long-term arrangement, but the pastor of Faith Center maintained that such an arrangement would not be satisfactory. As he pointed out, though we had black members, we were still perceived as a white church, and that created problems for them. He also admitted that our building was just too shabby for them, noting that how we cared for the building was an indication of how we cared for the church and one another, as well as the neighborhood. Though we thought his judgment a bit harsh about our physical "plant," his general point seemed right to us.

Acknowledging Who We Are

The next agenda item seemed to have more significant ecclesiological implications for those more attuned to theological issues. The worship committee had submitted a report recommending eucharist every Sunday. This report was the culmination of a long process in the church. Because the church had originally been evangelical, eucharistic practices had been rare. The new pastor, however, was liturgically conscious and had slowly increased the celebration of eucharist to once a month and then to most feast days, until finally the church was celebrating the eucharist almost thirty times a year. Indeed, one thing that attracted me to the church was the frequency of the eucharist.

The worship committee had drafted a paper on eucharistic practice in the church, which in particular dealt with John Wesley's views of the importance of frequent communion. The paper was distributed to the congregation, and a time was set to discuss it after service one Sunday. The discussion of the paper and our increasing celebration of the eucharist was positive. Issues such as whether too-frequent eucharistic practice might destroy its "special nature" were seen to be false. As was pointed out, the more the eucharist was served the more special it became.

The sense of the congregation had been developing over many years through the pastor's patient work. He was always candid about his hope that the congregation would want to move to eucharist every Sunday, but he never tried to force this on the congregation. Rather, through his preaching, his taking the eucharist to our many members in nursing homes and those too ill to come to the church, and in countless other ways, he helped us see how the eucharist made intelligible our care for one another and our communal life. I am sure that some people put up with the pastor's "high church views" partly because they had learned to love and respect him as a person who cared, but they also were learning that how he cared had much to do with the importance of the church's common work as determined by the eucharist. I should note that they were more than ready to oppose him on matters on which they thought he was wrong—thus despite his appeals to tradition, there was enough opposition that he was unable to have the front doors of the church painted red. As one member put it, "Oak grain ought to show."

The worship committee's suggestion that we move to eucharist every Sunday was thus not unexpected. The board discussed the worship committee's report in generally favorable terms. Anxious that the church move to eucharist every Sunday and feeling that the time was ripe for action, I moved that the next step be a vote to accept the report and its recommendations. There was general agreement that this would be appropriate, and so we prepared to vote.

We were, therefore, shocked when our pastor, who usually said little at our meetings, announced rather loudly, "You should not vote on this issue." My immediate reaction, and I suspect that of the others, was who the hell was he to tell us not to vote. After all, this was the duly constituted body of the church for governance, and we had every right to vote on this matter. Second, I thought the pastor had lost all his political sense. Here was a matter for which he had worked for years, coming to a vote that he clearly would have won, and yet he would not let us vote.

The pastor proceeded to explain that it was the church's norm that the eucharist be served every Sunday. For numerous reasons we had not been in accordance with this norm, which to him was unfortunate, but that did not give us the right to vote whether or not we would serve the eucharist. As he put it, we no more had the right to decide how often the eucharist would be celebrated than we did to decide whether we would say the Lord's Prayer every Sunday. Both were obligations that as a community we were invited to obey, or rather, they were privileges in which we ought to rejoice.

He then proposed, with the board's approval, a way that he would handle the matter. He would announce to the church that there was strong sentiment in the church to move to eucharist every Sunday. Recognizing that there might be some who disagreed with this policy, he would announce a time for them to come to express their disagreement. If many felt strongly that such a move would make it impossible for them to continue to worship with us, then we might have to wait a little longer. Not to wait, he pointed out, would belie the very unity we found in the eucharist. The board agreed. The meeting was called for two different times, but because no one came to either, we simply began having eucharist every Sunday.

Acknowledging Whose We Are

The board meeting ended soon after this decision, and the effects of that discussion as well as the subsequent eucharistic practice led to unexpected developments. It is generally assumed that Protestant churches that "go in for the high-church stuff" are rather well off and more aesthetically than socially aware. That such was not the case at Broadway I have already suggested by noting that the decision to reroof the education building occurred at the same time as the discussion about the eucharist. A further confirmation of the church's close connection between its eucharistic practice and its understanding of social mission came soon after.

About three months after the board meeting, the Outreach committee came to the church with another proposal. I should make clear that the people on this committee were not "special" in the sense that they had prior theological training. The chairman of the committee was an extraordinary layperson who had originally been assigned to the church during the Vietnam War to do community service as an alternative to being drafted, but the committee's proposal was not something that he alone wanted to do. Rather, the proposal reflected a consensus by the committee.

The Outreach committee's proposal began with its concern at being a church in a high unemployment area of a high unemployment city. The planned unemployment the Reagan administration had used to bring down inflation had hit South Bend particularly hard. Soup kitchens had begun to spring up in the city to feed the poor and unemployed, but somehow the committee felt that a soup kitchen, as much good as it might do, was not the church's principal mission. So the committee reminded the board that just as we had learned the significance of sharing a meal together, perhaps we could share a meal with the neighborhood. Such a meal would not be the same as the meal we share when Christ is the host, but at least it expresses the kind of community that such a meal has made possible. The committee thus recommended that every Sunday after worship the church have a lunch and invite anyone who wanted to come. We therefore would not so much feed the hungry as share a meal with them.

The board accepted the Outreach committee's proposal. The church was divided into five teams, each taking the responsibility for preparing the meal for one Sunday. At first the attendance was rather low, but as word got around, we often had between forty and sixty people at the Sunday lunch. A few who shared our meal came to church before the lunch, but we gained no new members from the effort. Yet that meal became central to the church's life, as it made clear that we were not simply another social agency that does a little good, but a people called out to witness God's presence in the world. The presence that comes in the meal we share sustained the church's ability to be present in the neighborhood as a symbol that all was not lost.

Christian Ethics and Seminary Education

So ends my story, though I obviously left out a lot and resisted telling the subsequent history of Broadway. [10] Telling more of the story, however, would not have helped me explain the unease felt by many regarding its possible implications. Some may have found the story interesting, and at least it seems to have had a happy ending, but what is the real point of telling it? What if anything can be made of this one incident in the life of this rather obscure congregation?

First, I think this story makes clear that the disdain of many theologians and ethicists for the "middle-class" church is unjustified. The story I have related is true. Although I did not describe in detail individual members of the congregation or the board, they are real people who work at the phone company, teach school, have babies, care for sick parents, and take time to come to church and attend meetings. Neither they nor Broadway are unique or special. What was done there is done in every church, and so I believe that churches that do not face the immediate challenge of survival can use their strength wisely. The crucial issue is whether the church is willing to trust that God is really present among us making us his church.

Second, this story questions some cherished distinctions that have shaped our reflection in Christian ethics. Is my account an example of a church or a sect type of ethic? Or is it an example of the "denomination," described by Gilkey, trying to recover some sense of its theological integrity? What such a story does, I think, is to remind us what we know but often forget, namely, that church, sect, and denomination are not descriptive but ideal types. They are not alternatives but, rather, heuristic devices that can help us better understand the empirical reality. In other words, they are the means to help us tell the story of a congregation like Broadway, not alternatives that determine our only options.

Yet too often, I think, we allow such categories to decide how we tell the

---

[10] For a fuller account of how narrative might prove illuminating for understanding as well as developing congregational life, see James Hopewell, "The Jovial Church: Narrative in Local Church Life," in *Building Effective Ministry*, 68–83.

story. For example, I think it would be a distortion of what was happening at Broadway to say that we were acting like sectarians. It is true that we were not trying to develop an ethic sufficient to sustain a civilization, but neither did we understand ourselves as "withdrawing" from the social order. Indeed, many in the church considered themselves as politically "conservative" and would be shocked at any suggestion that they were social radicals. It is also true that they understood that their first task as a church was to be faithful rather than effective. Yet that required us to be concerned about the neighborhood, and that concern meant that we had to care about what was happening in the politics of the city, and so on.[11]

Particularly important in this respect is the extraordinary range of activities in which the members of the church were involved. For example, some gave a great deal of their time to publishing and distributing *The Neighborhood News*. This small paper dealt with the good and bad news of the neighborhood and did much to give everyone a sense of common purpose. Some spent much time organizing fund-raising events for the church, such as bazaars and competitive road races. Such activities were meant not only to make money but also to attract people to the area who otherwise would have been afraid to venture into that part of the city. Some members took the time to attend city council meetings and became involved in local and state politics. And the list could be extended. What is remarkable is how people in the church appreciated each member's contribution, realizing that the diversity of activities contributed to what we were as a common people. Thus if the church was "sectarian," it was strangely so.

The sense of how the members' activities enriched the life of all, however, should not be limited to their social and political involvement. For as our pastor often reminded us, the church required our constant willingness to share with one another our particular stories. That does not mean that the church required all of us to "spill our guts," but rather, it became a place where our individual lives were enriched as we learned to share a history through our common worship. Such a history enabled us to appreciate the many paths that brought each of us to be a part of Broadway and thus one another. In the process we learned to value our differences as much as we rejoiced in our similarities.[12]

---

[11] It may be that my story only confirms Ogletree's observation that Christian ethicists ignore the church because the church, given its relegation to the private sector, no longer has "direct access to the great social questions of the day." Thus most Christian ethicists tend to be more comfortable dealing with denominationwide committees or commissions for social justice than with individual churches. Yet it is my contention that there is no greater social question for our day than the attempt to create the kind of viable community to which the people at Broadway were committed.

[12] I was pleased that members of the church took pride in knowing that a theologian from Notre Dame was a member, but they no less expected me to wash dishes after the lunch (because I could not cook I had to do something).

Yet although all this may be true, it still does not seem to contribute to our understanding of Christian ethics and/or seminary education. What difference does or should this story make for the role of the theologian? At the least I think that it reminds us that one of the theologian-ethicists's main tasks is to help congregations like Broadway appreciate the significance of their common acts. The way I have told the story of the board meeting is not the way that most who were at the meeting would have told it. They might not have seen the significance of reroofing the education building in the way I did; they would not have reported and interpreted the pastor's no to voting in the way I did. Even though my telling of the story clearly depends on my theological training, I know that the congregation would find my account helpful. For example, I told the story as we went through the process of finding a new pastor, and it helped remind us, and helped our new pastor understand, who we were.[13]

I am not suggesting that every church needs to have a theologian to help it discover the theological and ethical significance of its everyday activities. Indeed, given the convictions of many contemporary theologians, I cannot help but think that that might be disastrous for the church.[14] I suspect it would not be long before the churches would throw out the theologians—as did some Native American tribes that threw out the anthropologists whose interpretations, they felt, distorted their experience, and for much the same reason. Rather, I believe that it is the task of those committed to the theological enterprise to develop the linguistic skills that can help congregations better understand the common but no less theologically significant activities in their lives.

For example, the pastor at Broadway would sometimes tell us that every Sunday as he looked out at the congregation, which was often quite skimpy, he felt he was looking at a miracle. At first I thought that such language was exaggerated, but the more I thought about it, and the more Sundays I spent

[13] One of the issues raised by my emphasis on the congregation is the relation of the congregation to larger church structures. I think it fair to say that the United Methodist hierarchy of the Northern Indiana conference was not sure what to do with Broadway—what do you do with a United Methodist church that serves the eucharist every Sunday? If the focus on the congregation at least envisages some renewal of the congregation, then I believe that issues of the wider church's governmental structure in which that congregation exists cannot be avoided. Personally I have little confidence in church renewal from the top down. The best we can ask, and it is quite a lot, is for the denominational hierarchies not to hurt or impede local developments.

[14] I think that it is an indication of some of the deepest problems of modern theology that theologians are more shaped by their graduate school training than by their ecclesial identification, if any. Thus school designation, that is, whether one is a process thinker or a Barthian, is more determinative for how one works than whether one is Lutheran or Methodist. As a result, theologians tend to train ministers to make congregations fit the image of their particular theological allegiances rather than to help them respond to the congregation's past and present theological resources.

there, the more I became convinced that such words were appropriate. For there was no good reason that he or we could expect that anyone would be there, and yet we were there—diverse people who in many ways were strangers yet were joined in our determination to worship, convinced that through our presence to one another we were in the presence of God.

Thus I feel that no theology or ethic is truthful that does not help people, such as those at Broadway, appreciate the significance of their worship. Indeed, I suspect that much of the difficulty of current church life, and our corresponding theology, is that we have not paid enough attention to how difficult it is to understand the common things we do as Christians: pray, baptize, eat meals, rejoice at the birth of a child, grieve at illness and death, reroof church buildings, and so on. If we cannot describe theologically the significance of these activities, we will distort what we do by having to resort to descriptions and explanations all too readily provided by our culture. Any explanation is preferred to no explanation.

This process occurs at both crude and sophisticated levels. For example, when asked why they go to church, many people answer that it is there that they meet the kind of people they really like (people like themselves) or that there the kids learn morals. No doubt such explanations are part of the truth, but they may also be formulas for self-deception and lead us to miss the "miracle" that we are there to worship God. At a more sophisticated level we have learned to use sociological and psychological theories to explain the nature of the church. As a result, those trained to be ministers are often more adept at giving sociological accounts of church life than they are at helping their congregations appreciate that it is God who makes their life possible.[15]

I believe that one of the most promising ways to reclaim the integrity of theological language as a working language for a congregation's life is for seminaries to make liturgy the focus of their life. I do not mean simply that seminaries should have more worship services, though if done well that

---

[15] None of this is meant to deny the value of sociological, psychological, and general social-scientific accounts of the life of congregations. James Gustafson's *Treasures in Earthen Vessels: The Church As a Human Community* (New York: Harper Brothers, 1961) is still as relevant today as it was in 1961. The issue is the uncritical use of the social-scientific paradigms which often, if applied rigorously and consistently, methodologically preclude the theological claims necessary for the church's intelligibility. Two essays that help recapture the theological account necessary to understand a congregation's life are by Joseph Hough, Jr., and David Pacini in *Building Effective Ministry.* For example, Pacini suggested that behind many social-scientific accounts is the assumption that life is essentially mechanistic and so life processes take place according to predictable mechanical sequences. Fascinated with the power that such a model gives us to control, we concentrate on how social mechanisms function while ignoring our values, beliefs, and intentions. Moreover, we tend to assume that such a perspective is inclusive and all-embracing, thus failing to notice the extent to which it reflects our own notion of inclusivity. The use of such mechanistic metaphors in our secular culture, combined with claims of universality "reflects nothing other than the world view of the middle class, ordered by its penchant for management and its conviction that life processes are to be managed according to standards of predictability and lawlike generalizations" ("Professionalism, Breakdown, and Revelation," pp. 146–147). The issue is, therefore, not simply descriptive but normative.

might be helpful. Rather, I mean that the seminary's curriculum should be determined by and reflect the church's liturgical life. Why, for instance, should seminaries continue to teach courses in Old Testament and New Testament as if those were intelligible theological subjects? The scripture functions liturgically not as text but as canon. Yet in our classes we treat the scripture primarily as text, and then we who are responsible for training ministers are puzzled that scripture plays so small a part in the life of most Protestant congregations. Perhaps we should admit, in the words of Pogo, "We have met the enemy and he is us."

But if we recognize that such is the case, perhaps we can begin to respond creatively to the current malaise in seminary education. It is not as if those who specialize in scripture are more or less guilty than are those who work in theology and ethics. I suspect that the very distinction between theology and ethics reflects a failure to take seriously the liturgical life of congregations as essential to our educative task. It is perhaps a hopeful sign that many are attempting to recover liturgy as central to our theological work and that ethicists are discussing the liturgical shaping of the moral life.[16] But I do not think that we can be satisfied with these developments, as too often discussion about the relation of theology and liturgy is little more than an attempt by intellectuals to relieve the boredom of the current scholarly paradigms that determine their disciplines. Thus I fear that it may become just another "interest" of some intellectuals that will have the usual short run at the box office.

That is why my example of Broadway is so important. At the Broadway church I saw a congregation formed and disciplined by the liturgy in a way that made possible an extraordinary social witness. This congregation's life removes the distinctions between theology and liturgy, ethics and liturgy. The meal we prepare every Sunday for the neighborhood is not an expression of social ethical commitments distinct from liturgical life.[17] Rather, the meal and the liturgical life are parts of a single story. The theological task is first to help us and them understand why that is the case.

If it is to be productive, the emphasis on "the congregation" or "a congregation" for rethinking seminary education will require seminaries and their faculties to recognize that their legitimacy depends on how well they help bishops perform their duties.[18] The seminary's task is to train semi-

---

[16] Geoffrey Wainwright, *Doxology* (New York: Oxford University Press, 1980) is an outstanding example of a theologian working in this manner.

[17] I must now write in the third person, as I can no longer attend at Broadway, having moved to another city.

[18] Some may think that my reference to bishops in this context is too ecclesially specific. I debated whether to put the point in more neutral language, but I decided against it, as I think that the point I am making rightly notes one of the crucial bases for the office of bishop. Of course, I would not deny that a church without bishops may find persons and institutions who do not carry that name but in fact perform the task.

narians by telling the many stories of the congregations, past and present, that constitute the church of Jesus Christ—and that is also part of the bishop's task, as the bishop is the agent of the church's unity insofar as that office enables individual congregations to recognize that the life they share is also shared by other congregations. I suspect that is why, despite appearances to the contrary, New Testament and Church history courses often provide the most positive long-term help for people in the ministry, for it is in such courses that they learn about many "a congregation's" life.[19] As a result, they know that there are alternatives to the current stories of the church.

The task of Christian ethics is therefore the task of theology itself, to help the churches tell and share their stories truthfully. The normative implications of such truthful story telling can often be drawn as capably by church members as by Christian ethicists, as the following excerpts from a remarkable letter from one of Broadway's lay leaders attest. Just as the people at Broadway learned that they could and must share both their separate stories through their participation in the eucharist and the lessons outlined in this letter, so we theologians must continue that task. That does not mean that we are just story tellers, but it does mean that without stories—such as that of Broadway—all of our scholarship and intellectual skills would make little sense.[20]

> The purpose of my story is to tell you that the "minister as leader" model leaves me wanting something else. I would be much happier with the "minister as teacher and example" model. Please don't get my message wrong, I'm not blaming [the new pastor] for not being superman. I can, however, imagine a church where the people themselves adhere more closely to christian discipline and show greater faithfulness to their narrative than does the minister *and that situation is OK with the people*. In other words the minister-teacher would expect that his church would be the primary leaders in the local church. So, I'm praying that it was very right that we, the people, manage crisis, that we do it in a way consistent with the story, and *normally* without the leadership of a minister. Furthermore, when the minister is present in crisis he would

---

[19]Though often presented as an alternative to a "theological" approach to scripture, from this perspective the recent development of the "social world" methodology in the study of early Christian literature may be the most interesting theological development we have had for some time. See, for example, Wayne Meeks, *The First Urban Christians: The Social World of the Apostle Paul* (New Haven, Conn.: Yale University Press, 1983).

[20]I am indebted to John Westerhoff, Harmon Smith, Dennis Campbell, Michael Cartwright, Greg Jones, John Smith, and David Koehler for reading an earlier draft of this essay. I wish I had been able to respond to all their good criticisms and suggestions.

assume an equal role with the people and the people would not necessarily look to *his/her* wisdom to bail *them* out of a hard place. None of this makes any sense administratively, I am suggesting the virtual removal of what constitutes the cornerstone of many a congregation's structure. I want ministers to quit playing superman and quit taking full responsibility for the church as a captain takes responsibility for his ship. The people must minister to the people and learn the skills from the minister. Too often the outward character of the congregation is determined by the minister, a powerful leader, administrator and worker who tries to fill a void left by a vegetating congregation. The divinity school must start training congregations through its graduates. *The school must see its graduates as extensions of the school.* It seems to me that there would be a need for a professional journal published by the school and as free from denominational influence as is humanly possible. The teaching of ministers should not end with graduation. . . . I have but 3 primary areas of concern:

1. I'm worried that ministers will be transformed before congregations. I think you believe ministers can have profound influence on a congregation. But you do state somewhere that you see transformation happening first at the local church level. We are in agreement there. We need ministers who can tolerate congregations as they find them, just as we need lay persons with the same toleration. But the first order of business for both ministers and lay persons would be to have the congregation become active participants in salvation history and encourage others to follow.

2. There is not one activity of the church (BCP) that is crucial to our life together unless it be the Lord's Supper. Of course the soup lunch is different than most of the other ministries because it is done by the people and not by employees. I hope as time goes by the congregation will leave the endless chain of committee meetings and use their time in more activities like the soup lunch. We need leaders like [the chair of the Outreach committee] to make things like that happen. (Isn't he the kind of leader we need? If he were the minister he would be very much *less* effective [I really mean faithful] because he would be engulfed in irrelevant busy work. The thought occurs to me that we might be better off to have our minister work away from the church most of the week.)

3. Please spare me the "good, loving patient leadership" stuff. We need a person who knows what's going on (the story) and, by whatever style, draws us deeper into it. I was amused by your tale of the Parish Board when [the former pastor] would not let us vote on weekly communion. I think the really astonishing thing about the incident was that our good, loving, patient leader threw the Book of Discipline right through the oak grain doors and said "NO YOU DON'T." *And we didn't.*

But we, with his leadership, did act more consistent with our story. Let the styles fall where they may; give us people who know what needs to be done and the courage to do it. Can you give us ministers who can lead us away from dependence on their leadership?

TOWARD A CHRISTIAN FEMINIST LIBERATION HERMENEUTIC FOR DEMYSTIFYING CLASS REALITY IN LOCAL CONGREGATIONS

Beverly W. Harrison

Liberation Hermeneutics and the Reigning Theological and Social-Scientific Paradigms

I do not believe that Christian ethics is a discipline in either the classical or the modern sense of that term.[1] In my view, it is, rather, a high art form, a praxis,[2] that integrates—and must integrate—several streams of intellectual theory, themselves compounds of disciplines or heuristics of inquiry and interpretation.

To insist on this view of Christian ethics already signals that in mode and methodology I fall within the genre of liberation theology. This means that I understand all theory to be related dialectically to human experience and that I am committed to shaping my own theoretical choices in accordance with an active posture of resistance to domination.[3] Such resistance is not possible in isolation; it becomes a life option only in and through the experience of communities of resistance. It also acknowledges that such a vocation is to refuse dehumanization and to resist conditions that thwart life.

The streams of theory required to practice Christian ethics are (1)

---

[1] I do not understand Christian ethics to be a conceptually discrete body or system or knowledge, or a univocal theoretically informed heuristic of inquiry. Because Christian ethics is practical and moral, it is inherently evaluative and interdisciplinary. The point may seem banal, but in my opinion, much self-flagellation among professional Christian ethicists results from their inability to embrace enthusiastically the interdisciplinary character of their work.

[2] The normative force of insisting on a praxis conception of Christian ethics will, I hope, be clarified in what follows. I do not mean to suggest that Christian ethics should be praxis–based. My intent is to insist that all Christian ethics reflect at least a latent historical project, hence "a praxis."

[3] One of the most helpful expositions of what is involved in a hermeneutic of resistance to domination is found in the work of Elizabeth Schüssler-Fiorenza. See especially *In Memory of Her: A Feminist Reconstruction of Christian Origins* (New York: Crossroad, 1983), xiii–65; and *Bread Not Stone: The Challenge of Feminist Biblical Interpretation* (Boston: Beacon Press, 1985), 93–149.

theological theories of historical Christian[4] communities, (2) moral theories of both Christian communities and the cultural and intellectual traditions integrated into them, and (3) the various streams of social theory—the disciplines of human self-understanding that are, today, perceived as separate from Christian theological-ethical theory, including modes of social science, and also philosophical and scientific perspectives that have not otherwise been woven into existing Christian self-understanding by earlier integration.

Practitioners of Christian ethics today can develop a normative theory about what Christian ethics should be only through either an implicit or an explicit integration of these three strands. An explicit integration is preferable, because it makes clear one's assumptions. But every normative theological-ethical perspective is, simultaneously, a normative evaluation of theological-moral social relations.[5] Though I disagree with some of the theses advanced by David Pacini in an article on congregations, I agree with his dissent from the prevailing notion that theological investigations cannot arise from the analysis of social conditions:

> What is right about [this viewpoint] is the notion that there are distinctions between the analogies of social science and theology. What is wrong is the presumption that sociological analyses do not already contain an implicit theological viewpoint, or that theological analyses are not contingent upon an implicit sociological meeting.[6]

---

[4] Given the current theoretical and practical divisions in the Christian movement, I believe it wise to use the lower case when describing groups who identify with Christian traditions. I reserve the upper case for normative claims, what it should mean to be Christian. This does not imply that all Christian normative claims embrace the same belief-faith-praxis perspective. There are a number of Christian religious-political systems.

[5] Theories that conceptualize the human relationship to sacred power as running directly between God and believer or between God and church, without reference to nature, culture, or history/society often presume to live free of social-theoretical considerations. My perspective classifies such theologies as a species of capitalist social relations theory, even though this theological genre preceded the rise of a fully developed capitalist-political economic theory.

[6] David S. Pacini, "Professionalism, Breakdown and Revelation," in *Building Effective Ministry: Theory and Practice in the Local Church*, ed. Carl S. Dudley (San Francisco: Harper & Row, 1983), 134. I do concur with Pacini's call for more concern for metaphorical sensibility and with his unease with mechanistic notions of social process. I take such notions to result from "positivist" conceptions of science. However, I strongly disagree with the assumptions implicit in his "breakdown" thesis. I read him as informed by Alstair MacIntyre's idealist analysis of our malaise. What we are living through, in my view, are fundamental and humanly destructive institutional social-power realignments, largely invisible to us because of ideological manipulation. People do not just abandon or forget their cultural traditions or values. Rather, the communal forms of life that generate these traditions and values are crushed by a practice based on modes of power and rationality that decimate communities and their cultures. Of course, as a feminist I also cannot be a nostalgic cultural romantic like MacIntyre. Traditional culture also carries contradictions or socially embedded forms of domination. The resistance to struggle against racism and sexism rests precisely in this deep cultural embeddedness, and so a liberation hermeneutic also must be critical at the cultural level.

Though I would substitute the term *social* for *sociological* here, I concur that all notions of divine-human and human-human relations imply a conception of social relations and that all conceptions of social relations imply notions of what is benevolent cohumanity and sacred power. They also imply at least minimal moral notions about the obligations, values, and virtues[7] that should characterize human interaction. It is not possible to practice Christian ethics as a reflective action without an integrating of these theoretical streams.

None of us—seminary professors, social scientists, or lay Christians—can ignore the inclusive normative force of what we articulate, whether we speak of how we experience God or what we are to do in the church and world.[8] Furthermore, theology, moral theory, and social theory are embedded in ideological conflict, the fundamental human debate about the nature and direction of social change.[9] Christian ethics and the wider theological enterprise would be made clearer if more attention were paid to these epistemological issues.

My discussion pertains to the relationship of professional theologians to the life of congregations. Christian theologians and ethicists must accept, as they now do not, responsibility for forming their theories at the concrete loci of Christian praxis—local communities of believers. Like theologians, liberation theologians accept the normative character of theological-ethical reflection and do not claim to approach congregations disinterestedly. Unlike those who take other, more idealist positions, however, we assume the existence of resistance to domination in these communities. A liberation theological hermeneutic aims to enable members of the congregation to become more explicitly engaged in such resistance.

From a liberation perspective, what needs to be recognized is that the problem of many theologians' positions is not so much their excessive "accountability to the academy" per se. Rather, many inadvertently mimic reigning academic theories of knowledge, by embracing conceptions of theological truth that assume that Christian theology already has established and incontrovertible norms. As a result, the professional theologian's normative role becomes a protection against dissent. Theological theory is often appropriated idealistically, and the social context of praxis that produced it is forgotten. Rarely is the ideological role of past theological-ethical utterances made clear. Consequently, too many theologians join other academic elites in approaching the "object" of their research or the "subjects" of their consultation with much to teach and little to learn.

---

[7] I not only presume the desirability of attending to each of these traditional base points for a Christian ethic but also believe that no genuinely normative ethic is possible without addressing all three.

[8] I use the formulation church and world to make clear my own assumption, at the epistemological level, that our relationship to God is through nature-culture-society-history and that no one ever actually prescinds from this nexus. There is no Christ above the culture option.

[9] My point here is simply that there is no way for our theory to float free of "ideological entanglements." Self-awareness of an accountability for the ideological impacts of our work is the only road to the important, if modest, claims to objectivity we can ever justifiably make.

The difference between a liberation theological epistemology and the predominant ethos of academic theology is dramatic. Here I can identify only a few salient divergences. Although few dispute the appropriateness of normativity in theology, many dispute the locus of theological normativity. In a liberation hermeneutic, it rests not in confidence regarding the past theological truth but in the faith praxis of existing faith communities insofar as that faith praxis concretely transforms human life in the direction of nonalienating experiences of power and relations, of and to God, the world, and neighbor. Theology, like all humanly constructed perspectives, is here understood to function dialectically. It either masks or reveals power and relationships; it is life giving or it is life denying.[10] In its masking function, the theological perspective perpetuates and reproduces existing alienated relationships; and in its revealing function, it opens the way to realizing concrete good as shared power and a deeper relationship with God, world, and neighbor. According to this view, the concrete locus and generating center of all theology is in the particularity of people's real lives in their struggles. Appeals to orthodoxy as established truth do not admit the reception of fresh revelation or novel human experience. Theology ceases to be a self-critical discipline—one that can both challenge and unmask and incorporate new value as truth. The refusal itself of Christian theology to use resistance to oppression as the starting point, expecting new theological insight to arise from such a struggle, testifies to a nondialectical perspective on the relation of theory and praxis.

The literature on local congregations shows social science theorists capable of empathetic engagement with congregations and parishes, as even epistemologically inadequate theories of social science make some room for participation and empirical referents in their recommended modes of inquiry. I am not ready to change hats and cast my lot exclusively with the social theorists, however, because a liberation hermeneutic creates as deep epistemological differences with the reigning conceptions of social science theory[11] as with the reigning conceptions of theological-ethical theory.

I agree with many Latin American liberation theologians and embrace the radical conception of the role of social theory and science associated with a broadly Marxian view of human science.[12] That is, the aim of human

[10] In using the more typical radical conception of ideology here, I do not presume that there is a theoretical standing ground that ensures an ability to demystify. I believe that Marx is misread on this point, not only because of the misinterpretations of his view of science by conservative theorists like Karl Popper, but also because Marxist academic philosophers, especially of the genre of Paul Althusser, are attempting to return the Marxian tradition to the path of scientific positivism. Marxist academics, every bit as much as Christian theologians, seem incapable of bearing the *angst* that is required to live with the inherent contestability of human truth claims.

[11] Though I shall hereafter use the term *social science* to denote perspectives from academic fields, as differentiated from theology, I prefer the more complex formulation I use here, in order to avoid identifying my understanding of social science with empiricist notions of it.

[12] I do not mean to suggest that there is homogeneity in the interpretation and use of Marxism

science should not be to understand the world but to enable us to change it, and to do so with the aim of greater justice for members of our species and the wider environment in which we are set.[13] Marx is persistently misunderstood in the North American context, and so I insist that identifying with the Marxian genre of radical social science means denying that there can be any positive or noncontingent knowledge of the human social world and rejecting the view that there are "iron laws" in human history.[14] Radicals believe that the goal of social-theoretical inquiry is the greatest possible precision in comprehending how past social relations have enmeshed current human relationships in alienation and violence. From this perspective, human alienation is the result of exploitative social relationships. "Scientific" knowledge is a descriptive mode of "critical" knowledge, that is, knowledge that "unmasks" how the interpretations of the past are read to show that the social relations of the present cannot be changed. The test of "scientific" knowledge's adequacy, then, is whether it discerns the mechanisms of exploitation precisely enough to identify the patterns that must be altered in order for justice to occur.

Because theological and social-scientific theory must converge in a critical hermeneutic aimed toward justice (that is, mutual empowerment and right relationship), the theorist must understand his or her relationship to a community of believers not as didactic but as reciprocal. Critical theory, theological-ethical and social, must be tested and transformed in dialectical relation to the ongoing praxis and faith claims of other believers. In other words, my accountability as a theorist is to my own well-being and to those with whom I stand, and to what will happen to us in shared transformation as we struggle together for life-giving change. This does not mean that constructive social change is within our grasp or even possible in a given circumstance. A liberation hermeneutic presumes neither the simple malleability of our common life nor the amenability of existing alignments of power to genuine human fulfillment.[15] But it does posit the necessity of

---

in Latin American liberation theologies, only that they presume that social analysis must be made explicit in theological work and that the most genuinely historical-critical scientific perspectives should be used.

[13] I do not mean to suggest that Marx's own corpus is helpful in conceptualizing a notion of justice. It is not, in part, because Marx denied the possibility of an adequate moral theory under historical conditions of exploitation. Even if he had not, however, he was too preoccupied with analyzing the existing exploitation to reflect on the future. When concern for the future is neglected or suppressed, the dimension of ethical reflection is lost. The best treatment of Marx by a theologian, one that recognizes the point about Marx's failure to consider the future, is by Christopher Lasch, A Matter of Hope: A Theologian's Reflections on the Thought of Karl Marx (Notre Dame, Ind.: University of Notre Dame Press, 1982), 210–230.

[14] Marx's satirical uses of this phrase in discussing the "iron laws" of capitalism have been misunderstood by many theologians as defending positivist science, because they do not understand the political-economic view of Marx's contemporaries that he was challenging.

[15] I could emphasize this point by insisting on an uncompromising focus on domination and by

unending struggle for fulfillment and the godly presence that such a struggle promises. The proclamation of the divine promise of deliverance is truthful only when this struggle for shared, abundant life occurs. But such an annunciation is only mystifying double-talk without struggle. And this means that liberation theological rhetoric can mystify as much as any other can.

A Liberation Hermeneutic for Congregations

I can only roughly describe here the meaning of a liberation hermeneutic for the role of the Christian ethicist vis-à-vis the local congregation. One assumption of this hermeneutic is that its analytic point of departure must be the concrete life contradictions that operate in the church and the world to prevent human fulfillment. Over the last decade and a half, I have tried to locate and express solidarity with those local congregations whose entry point in this struggle has been resistance to the subjugation created by male supremacy in Christian tradition and praxis, a subjugation that renders women and their faith praxis all but invisible, whether in the literature on local congregations or their use (in which women are hardly a minority),[16] or in the images, metaphors, and narratives of theological confessions and liturgy. A feminist liberation theological hermeneutic, however, relates to more than gender relations: Feminist theory and struggle must answer to the oppression of all women and thus become a critique of all human domination in light of women's experience, a faith praxis that can unmask whatever threatens the well-being of the poorest, nonwhite woman.[17]

From a liberation stance, the guiding questions for congregational life are these: What contradictions deform the lives of those gathered in this community, and what forms does the resistance to these contradictions take? The patterns and structures of domination operate upon and within Christian communities, for a community of believers is never less or more than a community that shares the life of the world. But such a community may also—if it lives its praxis of faith—actively experience the divine presence in resisting disempowerment and alienation. Whether it does depends on the availability of critical resources, including theoretical ones, for demystifying

challenging any "scientific" reading of our situation that renders it resistant to a more adequate human praxis. A liberation hermeneutic breaks completely with the "progressivism" of any social theory that posits evolutionist enlightenment at the scientific, theological, or moral level.

[16] Barbara Wheeler observed the absence of women from the company of congregational researchers: *Building Effective Ministry*, 239. I am pointing to the even more notable absence of women from characterizations of the life of congregations and their surrounding communities and also in the conceptualizations of the social world used in these descriptions. What we have here is not merely a failure in human sensitivity but also a theoretically conditioned ineptitude.

[17] On this point, see The Mudflower Collective, *God's Fierce Whimsy: The Role of Feminism in Theological Education* (New York: Pilgrim Press, 1985).

domination. This is when theological, ethical, and social theory may help, not as a substitute for an ongoing praxis of resistance, but as an analytic component of this unmasking and annunciatory process. Communities of believers need the intellectual resources of theological-ethical-social traditions, not as imposed theory, but as a resource for a process that empowers them as agents of faith.

My experience working with the contradiction of gender among women in local congregations has taught me that the key to a liberation hermeneutic rests in a process of self-naming, or conscientization, whereby women learn to trust their own capacities as analysts and agents. Feminism has been a creative spiritual force in much mainstream Protestant congregational church life in the last fifteen years (and although male commentators have mostly missed this fact, it has been nearly the only dynamic spiritual force in predominantly white Protestant mainstream churches) because so many women have actually had this conscientization experience of empowerment. And despite the well-orchestrated effort to discredit feminist sensibility as a cultural and political force and to coopt women to reinforce traditionalist values, the spiritual health of any congregation can, more often than not, be measured by the changes taking place in women's roles.

My work with congregations has led me increasingly to the conviction that the major drawback to the presence of a liberation hermeneutic in local parishes, including the development of an inclusive feminist hermeneutic among the women in these churches, rests with the pervasive mystifications of other contradictions in congregational life. One, obviously, is the mystification of white supremacy. I do not know how to correct it in the predominantly white churches in which I work. My own conviction is that nothing works against the emergence of a genuine faith praxis among white Christian communities as much as does our failure to grasp the full meaning of "white privilege" on this planet at this juncture in history. At the same time, I believe that we cannot develop a faith praxis that resists white supremacy in its personal and political guises unless we discover far more about the particularity of the contradictions in our own lives. Using an inclusive feminist hermeneutic has deepened my conviction that insensitivity to others' suffering and to our own cultural destructiveness is conditioned by our failure to appropriate and accept the reality of our own pain and to comprehend how existing historical contradictions affect us. Because white Christians in the dominant culture have lost touch with the courage and struggle that have been part of our own heritage, a struggle that has grounded the most authentic values of that heritage, we neither see nor respect the contradictions and struggles of Afro-Americans, Latinos, Native

[18] See James Stolzman and Herbert Gamberg, "Marxist Class Analysis Versus Stratification Analysis As General Approaches to Social Inequality," *Berkeley Journal of Sociology* 18 (1973–1974): 105–125.

Americans, Asians, and others who are culturally marginal to the dominant ethos.

Accordingly, I have worked to develop a specific liberation hermeneutic process vis-à-vis white mainstream congregations that focuses on the contradictions most common in the lives of middle-American white people, whether in local communities of believers or in our wider common life. These contradictions and their attendant mystifications are related to the socioeconomic dynamics that shape our lives. Increasingly, I am interested in the possibility of conscientization with respect to the issue of class. What I propose to do in the space remaining in this paper is to clarify how a methodology might be conceived that aims at conscientization in class, a methodology formulated to enable local communities of believers to begin to name the alienations and disempowerments occurring in their lives today.

Toward a Critical Knowledge of Class Dynamics in Local Congregations

I do not accept most of the current characterizations of the socioeconomic situation of most mainstream local congregations and parishes. Nor do I believe that the fairly well educated rank and file of church members is equipped to revise social relations in this society. The privileged status of Christians is less a factor than most believe; more important is the identification of Christians and non-Christian "middle" Americans with the dominant ideology of the United States as "the promised land" and as a society characterized by "the individual as central sensibility."[19] By contrast, I believe that middle Americans live in a world in which we are growing more powerless to shape even local conditions of well-being. But should we identify with the dominant ideology, an identification that is secured in many ways? One characteristic of our life is a "social amnesia"[20] through which we lose touch with the particular struggles of our families and communities. Such an amnesia alienates us from anything in our present and past that does not correlate with the "American Dream" and upward mobility. Therefore we require a concept of class that resists reinforcing the dominant ideology.

Current social science blends the notion of class with social status and renders the concept heuristically empty by treating "class" as equivalent to "stratum," as in upper, middle, and lower. A stratified society permits the

---

[19]The term is Michael Lewis's, *The Culture of Inequality* (Amherst: University of Massachusetts Press, 1978).

[20]The term is from Russell Jacoby, *Social Amnesia* (Boston: Beacon Press, 1975). My own analysis of the sources of social amnesia does not follow Jacoby's, however. Invaluable resources for appreciating how a subjective appropriation of class injuries conditions this process are by Jonathan Cobb and Richard Sennett, *The Hidden Injuries of Class* (New York: Random House, 1972); and Lillian Breslow Rubin, *Worlds of Pain: Life in the Working Class Family* (New York: Basic Books, 1976).

mobility of some, but stratification, because it is viewed as inexorable, is of no historical import. Many factors—income, educational level, employment prestige—coalesce to create a class position, and a change of position results from a change in these factors. A more useful notion of class, however, does not merely identify stratum location but, rather, identifies what the concept of stratum location hides, namely, how socioeconomic dynamics enhance or prevent people's participation in shaping their lives and the life of their communities.

In teaching economic justice I have discovered that morally sensitive people, perhaps especially conscientious Christian people, have been encouraged to overlook their families' struggles for material survival, by identifying with some sector of the middle class. Having an adequate, even if moderate, family income is assumed to be a guaranty of middle-class status, and an income of $60,000 for a family of six that enables the parents to own a home and two cars and to pay the full costs of private higher education for the children is interpreted as affluence. Not infrequently, students in my seminary classes acknowledge that coming to appreciate the dynamics of the global and the U.S. economy has led to reconciliation with their parents, whose anxieties about money they had previously written off as greed! When I ask my students to locate more relevant indices of class—in either their family's income-producing wealth or their power to determine the goals of their work, few claim an upper status of any kind.

When a stratum-status notion of class prevails, a social theorist can characterize a congregation's class status by determining the group's average income and other relevant factors. The literature on congregations abounds in such characterizations and also the assumption that a given congregation is homogeneous at the social-economic level. To be sure, most mainstream, predominantly white congregations or parishes are homogeneous in one sense: Most of the members of a given congregation belong to the same statistical class stratum. But I submit that a critical consciousness, one that is aware of contradiction and mystification, requires us both to be suspicious of the dominant liberal theory of class and to fear the further repression of particularity that follows from any easy diagnosis of homogeneity.[21] If empowerment lies in the simultaneous recovery of both particularity and deepened relationship, do we dare to analyze congregations in this way?

The prevailing theory of class has other problems. A stratum-status analysis by family units, for example, hides women's economic vulnerability. The full-time homemaker is always economically vulnerable, as high poverty rates among recently divorced homemakers attest. (Conclusions about the homogeneity of congregations usually leave women out of the picture al-

---

[21] I do not mean to say that objectivistic-scientific description does not provide valid information. What it does not do is clarify pastoral strategies for helping people avoid "class injury" by not internalizing the dominant ideology.

together. A woman pastor told me that the percentage of older widows in her upper-middle-class congregations who, for financial reasons, lived on cat food is staggering.) Furthermore, family income figures invariably mask the deep differences in male income levels in apparently similar, but actually different, "white collar employment." Most families have "middle incomes" because two salaries, not one, are involved. There are other objections to the stratum-status theory. More to the point, however, is that its emphasis on income masks rather than reveals the basic questions that concern for "class" should foster: Who controls the resources shaping our lives, and who participates, or is excluded from participation, in socially generated power? Both men's and women's lives are mystified and misrepresented by a stratum-status analysis. Increasingly, this mystification is the one that most threatens the spiritual integrity of congregation life.

I cannot outline an alternative theory of class here. But as in so many other analytic matters,[22] I agree with Karl Marx that classes are antagonistic groups created by the patterns of social relations conditioned by the organization of the social means of production.[23] Marx insisted that society's organization of the means of production would affect social relations more directly than would other factors because material well-being is so basic to species survival. Such organization will most directly determine the extent to which a society's social fabric is characterized by alienation. Unless human sensuous labor joins control of the goals of production, exploitation will be intense. To demystify this exploitation, the relationship of work, ownership, and control must be seen in historical perspective.

Marx's insight that economic activity is principally human work—not, as in capitalist economic theory, the buying and selling of goods and the exchange of money—is critical to an adequate theological method.[24] Even though we now live in a capitalist global political economy, in which most labor (an exception is household work) is turned into a commodity—some-

[22] For other reasons to prefer a broadly Marxian approach to social theory, see "The Use of Social Theory in Christian Ethics," in Beverly W. Harrison, ed. Carol S. Robb, *Making the Connections* (Boston: Beacon Press, 1985).

[23] "Means of production" here means the total complex of land, resources, human labor, and machines needed for any society to produce "surplus value"—more value than those resources had before they were used in a productive process. At the risk of either tediousness or tendentiousness in the interpretation of Marx, I want to remind my readers that he neither objects to private ownership of personal property nor implies that markets have no place in a democratized economy. We have no more business holding Marx responsible for the idiocies of some of his followers that we do holding Jesus responsible for the crimes of some of his.

[24] It cannot be overstressed how thoroughly we are imbued with the capitalist understanding of the role of economic reality in human life. Even thoughtful efforts to make churches and Christians concerned about economic morality can reinforce this neoclassical paradigm. I have commented on how the Pastoral on Economic Life of the National Conference of Catholic Bishops does this, in "Social Justice and Economic Orthodoxy," *Christianity and Crisis* 44 (January 21, 1985). It should also be noticed that the bad habits of many Christian ethicists in spending most of their energies on questions of distributive justice rather than on communicative justice also reinforce the fallacies of the neoclassical economic paradigm.

thing we do in order to make money—it is still important to consider the theological-ethical significance of the nature and quality of people's work as basic to their spiritual and moral well-being. It is all the more important at a time when life in the workplace is deteriorating for everyone and the prospects for meaningful work for most people are eroding.

Marx's class analysis of early industrial capitalism clearly has been preempted by the dramatic changes in the now-global capitalist system.[25] The antagonistic and exploitative relations that Marx identified in the middle-period capitalist Europe between the owners of the means of production and the wage laborers they employed continue to generate conflict wherever capitalist modes of production are introduced into a society. At the heart of the late global capitalist system, however, structural realignments in the political economy are only one conflict in the owners' (transnational corporations) exploitation of wage laborers.

The newer dynamics of exploitation relevant to the daily life of middle Americans in congregations include capital shifts, via the corporate state, that are making obsolete all decentralized economic life. That is, small independently owned businesses and farms and small, locally based corporations are becoming untenable or are maintained as costly ventures in family loyalty to local communities. Everywhere large industries capitalize only very profitable ventures. Industrial leaders make decisions without reference to whether the nation's manufacturing base is secure enough to provide the machine tools needed. Exceedingly profitable high technology shapes life in the workplace. New jobs, when they are created, are either high-income, high-technology positions or insecure, low-wage, service-sector positions.[26] The national budget is slashing expenditures for education, social programs, and human welfare expenditures in order to increase high-technology military production. Moral questions aside, the increased military expenditures provide only a few jobs per number of dollars expended. Government welfare functions are increasingly being returned to the private sector. Our national leadership disguises this counterrevolution against the modest gains achieved by earlier political struggles for justice with a rhetoric about private charity and the erosion of traditional values.[27] Such language manipulates

[25] Unless we connect the analysis of our national economy's dynamics with global structural dynamics, we may also reinforce the wave of nationalistic fervor now orchestrated to discourage dissent. In 1975, a young Latin American economist said to me, "You in North America face a much more difficult task than we do; you must get people to see the direct connections between the sufferings of your people *and* those of Peruvian peasants." I mark that conversation as the origin of my own participation in economic ethics.

[26] An excellent reflection on this matter is by Alan Geyer, "Politics and the Ethics of History," *Annual of the Society of Christian Ethics, 1985*, ed. Alan B. Anderson (Washington, D.C.: Georgetown University), 3–17.

[27] William A. Tabb, "The Social Political, and Ethical Meaning of the Reagan Revolution," *The Annual of the Society of Christian Ethics, 1983* (Distributed by CSR, Waterloo, Ontario), 185–216.

the fears and nostalgia of people who do not comprehend what is happening. Because they are identified with an amorphous middle stratum or status, Christians are as susceptible as is everybody else to this rhetoric, especially when political leaders ritually embrace those Christian leaders and groups who most often turn theology and ministry to the service of celebrating "tradition."

All this is affecting the daily life of every person in every Christian parish and is placing incredible pressures for conformity on the congregations themselves. At best, we have only a few components of an analytic approach that can help Christian people comprehend this situation.

My work with local church people has taught me that their resistance to examining these issues has less to do with political ideology and identification than with their mistrust of the church as the sort of community in which such revelation may occur. The laity and clergy both feel this mistrust, for very different reasons. Furthermore, my feminist commitment has led me to deal simultaneously with gender and sexuality and with economic justice and class in my work with clergy and laity. As a result, my work with congregations has revealed that sex and money are taboo subjects in the parish because nearly everyone feels vulnerable to them. Very few believe that as experienced in their congregation, Christian love includes attention to people's suffering in these areas. In order to overcome this mistrust, the development of a critical consciousness of class issues requires participation and mutuality at all levels of congregational life.

The ability to develop a critical class consciousness is not much affected by a congregation's theological perspective. Self-identified liberal congregations and clergy usually have a strong, historically conditioned resistance to accepting struggle and conflict in the community, and far more powerful mechanisms operate within such congregations to identify with the dominant cultural ethos. The social amnesia characteristic of "middle-stratum-identified" groups is especially prominent in liberal churches because job mobility and education obscure connections with family roots. Conservative churches are not much different.

I am still hopeful that approaches to developing a critical class consciousness will emerge from the personal narrative on which a liberation hermeneutic depends. In my work, I use both social and personal cross-generational narratives of individuals and their families and historical narratives about socioeconomic changes in the United States. I then ask the participants to trace the theological-ethical-social biography of their own families across at least three, and if possible, five generations. I ask them to record the socioeconomic factors, cultural sensibilities, and religious convictions, praxis, and observance of past generations of their families. I have them describe the geographic location and type of homes the family occupied, their personal possessions, the work they did, and their access to and attitudes toward money, education, and social status. I ask them to look at patterns of gender relations in their families and how their situations related to the profiles of neighbors in the communities where they lived. I urge them to explore the effect of all these factors on their families' piety and religious practice. In reconstructing their stories, I have my students note experiences of poverty, deprivation, and natural disaster, struggles against illness, personal and social tragedies, and the positive values that helped them in these struggles.

Not surprisingly, this assignment, even when carried out over a period of time that allows for digging and research, confronts participants with a dramatic map of their own and their families' collective social amnesia. Frequently, the result is the discovery that families seem to remember only their "successes" and to forget the "failures." Often relatives' personal problems, such as educational failures, family violence, divorce, and alcoholism, are related to indices of downward socioeconomic mobility, a relationship that no one in most families ever considered when dealing with those who were "problems."

When the narratives have been reconstructed and shared with the other participants, I ask the group to relate their familial-personal narratives to a broader critical analytic one, drawn from the work of historians and political economists who share neither the "promised land" reading of U.S. history nor the myth of perpetual upward mobility. The narrative I use shifts somewhat from group to group. Among rural congregations, I highlight the history of U.S. agriculture and the impact of business cycles and government policy on farmers, as well as the cultural impact of urbanization on rural cultural and social life. With urban congregations in the Northeast, I highlight the effect of central capitalist institutions such as banks and corporations on urban centers as well as their role in deindustrialization. In every historical narrative, I describe the effect of war and government policy on veterans, education, land and resource use, and labor.

From these sessions, I have learned that many clergy and laypersons are familiar with the history of their communities and regions but that they understand only little about the impact of national governmental policy. (This is an index, I suspect, of how little they fear the long-term consequences of our current administration's actions.) Few appreciate how much presumed social mobility, in nearly all families, is tied to shifting government policies and to government activism in social welfare. A few examples will suffice: Most autobiographical narratives highlight two points in a family's pilgrimage: the beginning of educational achievement and the first ownership of land or a home. Both are perceived as the crossing of a class threshold. What most people do not realize is that home or land ownership for most American families is made possible by either government land grants or low-interest housing loans for veterans. Except for those who enjoy corporate or more affluent professional income levels, home ownership is chiefly enabled by inheritance, a pattern likely to become more common in the future.

Higher educational levels are also related closely to state and federal policies, but by examining the differences between their parents' educational experience and their own and their children's, participants learn that education by itself is no longer a guaranty of upward mobility. Thus, the so-called conservatism of the young and their demand that education respond to the job market is interpreted by some as the result of greed; but these demands are in fact responses to objective and destructive social conditions. A further insight has emerged. What most families experience as periods of upward mobility correlate closely with periods of expansion in the United States economy, especially those following World Wars I and II. That our economic system has become slightly more equitable only when other industrial economies have been decimated by war comes as a shock to most people.

I cannot say much about the broader significance of this sort of conscientization for the ongoing life of congregations. In most instances, this process precipitates a deeper interpersonal respect and a greater ability to identify the roots of powerlessness. Whether such an approach can lead some in the congregation to concern for the well-being of the wider community remains to be seen.[28] What is clear is that for the clergy and laity, the resulting self-respect is not simply personal. It embraces their family forebears, whose life and struggles take on new meaning and power. Their growing capacity to perceive and analyze social dynamics transforms once private pains into public issues with intersubjective grounding in the dynamics of the current political economy. I do believe that those clergy, seminarians and lay people equipped to engage in this sort of hermeneutical process become more able to relate to what is going on in their congregations. As a result, some have reoriented their pastoral work.

I am not hopeful about the prospects for widespread adoption of this sort of liberation hermeneutic in the life of middle-stratum churches in the United States. Yet I see no alternative except to press on with this process. Such engagement has priority for me as a practitioner of feminist Christian liberation ethics, not because of any particular theological-social theory, as much as I value the theory and practice I have developed. Nor is this priority based on the expectation of success. Rather, it is grounded in my acceptance that these white, Christian middle-stratum folk in the mainstream churches are my people. Like me, my people are capable of empowerment in God as they develop a praxis of justice. Making the connections between my own and others' struggles has also taught me a harder truth; namely, that lacking

---

[28] Obviously, a movement beyond conscientization and initial analysis to reorienting our broader praxis depends not merely on deepening the life of the congregation but also on making connections with those in the broader community whose praxis is convergent. Because this society is in a situation of severe political repression, such linkages are difficult to make. We must learn to respect the long-term scope of our struggle. Although the prospects for progressive regional and national strategies are dim at present, I believe that new possibilities are emerging locally, if we could only see them.

such empowerment, we pious, white, middle-stratum people in this nation are dangerous to those who share the planet with us. Professing ourselves particularly blessed and truly free, when we are neither, robs us of the capacity to fight for our own lives and also to see and respect the courage, creativity, and transformative power of those many others who struggle for theirs. A liberation hermeneutic in the mainstream churches is a nonnegotiable requirement, not to return these churches to the position of cultural hegemony they once enjoyed, but to ensure that the rising tide of "friendly fascism"[29] in our midst will not be able to claim a sanctified Christian face.

[29] The phrase is from Bertram Gross, *Friendly Fascism* (Boston: South End Press, 1983).